MEMORIES OF THE LAKES

Told in Story and Picture

MEMORIES OF THE LAKES

Told in Story and Picture

BY

DANA THOMAS BOWEN

FRESHWATER PRESS, INC.

1700 E. 13th Street - Suite 3 R

Cleveland, Ohio 44114

ISBN: 0-912514-14-0

CONTENTS

CONTENTS (CONT.)

⚓ ⚓ ⚓ ⚓ ⚓ ⚓ ⚓ ⚓

ILLUSTRATIONS

ILLUSTRATIONS (Cont.)

ILLUSTRATIONS (Cont.)

XIII

⚓ ⚓ ⚓ ⚓ ⚓ ⚓ ⚓ ⚓

DEDICATION

To the first listener to my many nautical tales, to my partner in so many of my maritime adventures, to my manuscript critic, to my galley proof editor, to my inspiration to accomplish better things, and to my devoted wife, Lois, who is all these and so much more to me, I dedicate this book on the twenty-fifth anniversary of our signing articles.

Dana T Bowen

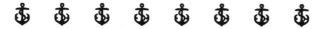

PREFACE

The complete history of the Great Lakes will, of course, never be told. Many volumes have been written and many more may be forthcoming, but all the detailed history of these great bodies of fresh water can never be recorded. Every mile of shore line has its own story, as has every ship. Many men and ships have long since passed from the beautiful shores of these lakes and their valiant stories are buried with them.

Today we can only retell those tales that have been handed down to us by letter and word. A few men still live who can talk first hand of actual experiences aboard the bygone windjammers of the lakes, and of those early struggles of the creaking wooden steamers to gain a foothold in the realm of commercial transportation.

It has been the author's pleasure to search out many of these old sailors and to listen to their adventures. Every available old book and record pertaining to the subject has been carefully studied. The maze of material is astounding from which to make the selections of the most interesting stories. The years gone by have piled up wondrous tales, and herein is a modest attempt to retell only a few of them. That they may be as fascinating to the reader as they were to the author is the purpose of this book.

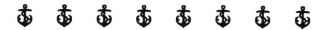

A WORD OF EXPLANATION

This is the second book written by the author on the Great Lakes. The first was LORE OF THE LAKES, published in 1940.

This book does not attempt to make either a complete or a chronological recording of the history of the Great Lakes. It is rather a scrapbook collection of historic tales of the lakes and their ships, written as they came to mind. Many are retold from personal interviews.

MEMORIES OF THE LAKES has avoided that which is told in LORE OF THE LAKES. It is intended that the two books be considered the beginning of a series on the same subject. The author hopes to continue this series with more of the interesting high lights of Great Lakes lore.

⚓ ⚓ ⚓ ⚓ ⚓ ⚓ ⚓ ⚓

CHAPTER ONE

DID YOU KNOW THAT . . . ?

. . . . A brig of 96 tons was built for service on Lake Erie in 1814, but was shortly laid up as being too big to successfully handle the trade. One of the latest ships built on Lake Erie, the *Irving S. Olds,* is of 14,500 tons and is quite successful in her trade.

. . . . The St. Lawrence River was discovered by the explorer Aubert in 1508. The French explorer Jacques Cartier ascended the St. Lawrence as far as the Indian village of Hochelaga, now Montreal, in 1534.

. . . . Lake Huron was the first of the Great Lakes to be discovered by the white man. Some historians claim that the French explorers Le Caron and Champlain both discovered Lake Huron in 1615, but in separate parties. They state that both explorers came up the St. Lawrence as far as Montreal and then up the Ottawa River. Then different routes across country were taken toward Georgian Bay and Lake Huron. The exploring parties are said to have met in the Lake Huron region and joined forces.

. . . . Lake Ontario was discovered the same year, 1615, on their return to Montreal.

. . . . Lake Superior was discovered in 1629 by the French explorer, Brule.

MEMORIES OF THE LAKES

. . . . Lake Michigan was discovered in 1634 by the French explorer, Nicolet.

. . . . Lake Erie was the last of the Great Lakes to be discovered, though geologists claim it to be the oldest. Joliet discovered it in 1669.

. . . . In 1812 a small sailing vessel, the *Fur Trader,* was built on Lake Superior. After being used in the fur trade a short time, an attempt was made to run her down over the rapids at St. Mary's Falls to get her into the lower lakes. She was almost completely wrecked in the attempt. Later, in 1817, another little vessel, the *Mink,* was successful in running the swift rapids, sustaining but little damage. The rapids have almost vanished at present, only a trickle of water flows over the rocky floor.

. . . . Lake Superior country is the locale of the famous legend poem Hiawatha written by Henry W. Longfellow. Information and story was given him by Henry Schoolcraft, the American historian of Indian lore who lived in Sault Ste. Marie, Michigan, and served there as the Indian Agent for the government in the early days of the nineteenth century.

. . . . Sandusky Bay has an island that comes and goes. It is called Spit Island and is located near the mouth of the bay where it enters Lake Erie. In 1821 it was a promising vacation spot, some fifteen feet above water and held some fine trees. Then it started to sink. Piling was put in to save it. The piling went down with the island, as did the trees. Lake Erie washed over Spit Island and placed it under six to ten feet of water. Later years Spit Island rose from the depths and was again above normal water. Grass grew and pleasure boat parties enjoyed picnic suppers on the up and coming Spit Island. As this is written, Spit Island has once more disappeared from the surface of the lake and has about five feet of water over it.

. . . . Port Huron was once known as Desmond; Saint Clair as Palmer; Marine City as Newport, and Algonac as Manchester.

. . . . In 1850 there were 820 commercial sailing vessels on the Great Lakes. Twenty years later there were 1,445.

. . . . The Sturgeon Bay Ship Canal connecting Lake Michigan and Green Bay was begun July 8, 1872, and on June 28, 1878, the waters from both ends met. Small craft were then able to use the canal, but it was not declared fully completed until the fall of 1881, when large vessels were able to navigate the waterway. It is nearly ten miles in length and has no locks.

. . . . The combined area of the Great Lakes exceeds that of England, Scotland and Wales.

. . . . The Steamer *United States* was navigated throughout the entire winter of 1845 between Buffalo and Detroit by Captain Harry Whittaker. This was never done before that year nor since.

. . . . Before the advent of the modern type of steam freighter on the Great Lakes, and while the windjammers were supreme, the tug towing business naturally flourished. Competition was extremely keen. Rival harbor tugs would race each other out into the open lake to meet an incoming

7

schooner for the business of towing her into port. Tug crews vied with each other, and all sorts of questionable practices were resorted to; firemen's coal shovel handles were secretly partly sawed through by rival firemen, causing them to break off when used. The red and green lights on a tug hurrying to meet a schooner at night would be reversed, causing their compeitors, at a glance, to suppose the tug to be heading in the opposite direction. Not unusual was it for tugs to go the whole length of Lake Huron, from Port Huron to the Straits of Mackinac, and occasionally all the way to Escanaba, to assemble a tow of schooners to bring down through the St. Clair and Detroit Rivers.

. . . . A pipe organ was installed in the big bulk freighter, *Wilpen,* for the entertainment of her invited guest passengers, when she was built in 1907. It was subsequently removed.

. . . . Vessels loaded in the fresh water of the Great Lakes and passing into the salt water of the oceans will rise up to six or seven inches upon entering the ocean.

. . . . Old timers about the Great Lakes all talked about "Chicken Bone Reef," but no one had ever seen it, and no chart showed it, but any sailor would tell you that it was in the Detroit River just off Woodward Avenue. It was here that the government Revenue Cutter *Fessendon,* and the Navy Gunboat *Michigan,* and others, used to anchor for long times. Ordinary merchant sailors claimed that "Chicken Bone Reef" was built up from the river bottom by all the chicken bones that were thrown overboard from the tables of the ships anchored there.

. . . . Pottawatomie Lighthouse on Rock Island, Wisconsin, built in 1837, is believed to be the oldest light structure still in use, and unchanged since its original construction, according to a Coast Guard officer.

. . . . A submarine was on Lake Michigan as early as 1845. It was built at Michigan City, Indiana, by a twenty year old named Lodner Darvontis Phillips to salvage sunken treasures. It was not a success and sank during early tests, with no loss of life.

. . . . 1945 was the Fiftieth Anniversary of the Detroit River Floating Post Office, only one of its kind serving passing ships.

. . . . An Englishman interested himself in safety aboard ships. In 1876, through his efforts, he had legislation passed that required a load line to be painted on the sides of ships. The man was Samuel Plimsoll, and today his "Plimsoll Mark" is on every registered commercial ship on the Great Lakes and throughout the world. It is a peculiar set of markings on the sides of a vessel, placed there after scientific study, to denote the depth to which she may be safely loaded. The "marks" remain on the ship as long as she is in service. These various lines indicate the safety for full loading in different seasons of the year, and in different waters and parts of the world. In detail, the Plimsoll Load Line is a circle 12 inches in diameter, with a horizontal line 18 inches long painted through its center. Twenty-one inches forward of the circle's center is a vertical line which is joined at right angles by other lines 9 inches in length, which indicate the maximum load at various seasons and conditions. The lines extending toward the bow refer to salt water operation, while the line aft is for fresh water service. Each line has a letter painted for it. They read top to bottom: "FW" for Fresh Water; "IS" for Indian Summer (Salt Water); "S" for Summer (Salt Water); "W" for Winter (Salt Water); and "WNA" for Winter, North Atlantic.

. . . . Free Marine Hospital medical service for all seamen dates back to 1884. Prior to that a tax of forty cents per month was levied for each seaman belonging to the crew of an American vessel to cover such service.

. . . . There are reported to be 1,692 islands in the Thousand Islands. There are over 30,000 islands in the Georgian Bay group.

. . . . Stannard Rock Lighthouse is the most isolated lighthouse on the Great Lakes, and marks one of the most dangerous reefs in Lake Superior. It is also one of the highest, being 102 feet above the water. Stannard Rock, upon which the light is built, is not much larger than a fishing dory turned upside down. It was first lighted on July 4, 1882. It was named for its discoverer, Captain Charles C. Stannard, who sailed early vessels on Lake Superior. Captain Stannard died "at the bells" aboard the steamer *Western World* as it left Detroit on one of its regular trips in 1856.

. . . . Fresh water ice floats in fresh water with one-tenth of its mass above water. Salt water ice in salt water has one-ninth above water.

10

DID YOU KNOW THAT . . . ?

. . . . Port and Starboard—grand old seafaring words—are gradually being placed in the background. They are being superseded by what they actually mean—left and right, respectively. This is how the odd names came into the maritime vocabulary in the first place. Very early salt water sailing ships were maneuvered by a so-called "steering board" which was hinged to the right side of the hull, the principle being somewhat similiar to the manner in which an oarsman controls a canoe. The right side of a ship gradually became known as the "steerboard side." This was later abbreviated to "starboard side." "Port side" comes from the fact that ships of the 17th century could be loaded from but one side—the left, as they had only one loading port on the ship. This side became known as the "ladeboard side," which later was "larboard side." Difficulty then arose because of the similarity of the two, so the sailors dropped the "larboard" and called it "port."

. . . . There is a shoal spot almost in the middle of Lake Huron where the depth is about six fathoms. There is also a shoal spot in Lake Superior, near Stannard Rock Light, where the depth is about seven fathoms.

. . . . A Great Lakes passenger steamer once carried iron ore. The cargo was loaded by wheelbarrows on the freight deck of the steamer *Japan* in 1871. This cargo is said to have made the first Bessemer steel in America.

. . . . In 1879 the prevailing salary paid to reliable Great Lakes passenger steamer masters was about $1,300 per year.

. . . . A Great Lakes captain sailed for twenty years (1860 to 1880) and never had a chart in his hands. He

11

was Captain Alexander McDougall, inventor of the whaleback type of ship.

. . . . The following comment is taken from the Holy Bible. "They that go down to the sea in ships, and occupy their business in great waters; these men see the works of the Lord, and his wonders in the deep." It is contained in Psalm 107: 23-24.

. . . . It is an old maritime tradition on Christmas Day aboard ship, to lash a Yule tree to the mast. This custom is still followed by many shipmasters of modern times.

. . . . Lake Superior seldom gives up its dead, particularly in deep water. The water is so cold that bodies do not decompose and consequently do not rise to the surface.

. . . . The name "Coast Guard" was officially applied to that service in 1915, after merger of the Revenue Cutter and Life Saving Services. The Lighthouse Division was not included until 1939.

. . . . The Coast Guard normally is under the U. S. Treasury Department. The custom of transferring it to the Navy during wartime was established during the undeclared war against France, which ended in 1801.

. . . . The Temporary Reserve of the Coast Guard, made up entirely of civilians, is the only organization of its kind in the nation's military history. It was organized in 1942 and members were disenrolled late in 1945.

. . . . The eagle adorning caps of Coast Guard officers faces right, toward the wearer's sword arm, the heraldic position of honor.

12

DID YOU KNOW THAT . . . ?

. . . . The St. Clair Flats Ship Canal, which has no locks, was completed in 1871.

. . . . Sound travels at the rate of 1,090 feet in a second, when the temperature is at the freezing point, and about 1,125 feet when the temperature is 60 degrees above zero (Fahrenheit).

. . . . The greatest depth of water in the Great Lakes is in Lake Superior, 168 fathoms, at a point 53 miles NNE¼E from Manitou Island Light, and 61 miles E½S from Passage Island Light.

. . . . The greatest depth of water in Lake Michigan is 145 fathoms, at a point 26½ miles SW by W ½ W from Point Betsy Light, and SE by E ¼ E, 33½ miles from Sturgeon Bay Ship Canal Light.

. . . . The greatest depth of water in Lake Huron is 125 fathoms, at a point 26½ miles SSW ¾W from Cove Island Light, and 58 miles E¼S from Thunder Bay Island Light.

. . . . The greatest depth of water in Lake Erie is 35 fathoms, at a point 6½ miles SE ⅛E from Long Point Light, and N by E ⅛ E, 24½ miles from the main light at Erie.

. . . . The greatest depth of water in Lake Ontario is 123 fathoms, at a point 28 miles NE by E ⅛ E from the pierhead light at Charlotte, and NNW ¼ W 15½ miles from the main light at Big Sodus.

. . . . The greatest known depth of water in the world is near the island of Guam in the Pacific Ocean. This sounding is 5,269 fathoms, or nearly six statute miles.

13

MEMORIES OF THE LAKES

. . . . At one time there were more than two hundred harbor tugs in the port of Bay City, Michigan. Now there is not a single one, although the tonnage in and out of that port now exceeds the tonnage of the tug days.

. . . . Regular lake passenger service was established to Chicago in 1830.

. . . . Spectacle Reef Lighthouse in northern Lake Huron is one of the greatest marine construction projects in the United States. It cost nearly one-half million dollars.

. . . . A light one hundred feet above lake level can be seen under normal conditions approximately thirteen miles.

. . . . The Great Lakes Industrial Region produced one-third of the equipment for the invasion of Europe in World War II. Over sixty-one billion dollars worth of combat equipment and munitions were delivered into the hands of the United Nations for the invasion.

. . . . Most of the cities located on the shores of the Great Lakes take their water supplies from the lakes.

. . . . The United States Lake Survey was instituted March 3, 1841, when Congress made its first appropriation. The first lake charts were issued in 1852. These were: a chart of Lake Erie, a chart of the West End of Lake Erie, and a chart of Kelleys and Bass Islands. By 1882 the first comprehensive series of charts of the Great Lakes had been published.

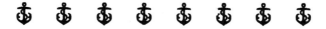

Chapter Two

GREAT LAKES FIRSTS

The first white man to see Niagara Falls is believed to have been the explorer Brule who, in 1629, discovered Lake Superior.

The first recorded passage of the Detroit River by white man was in 1670 by two French priests.

The first vessel on the Great Lakes was the *Griffin,* of 60 tons, built by the French explorer, La Salle, at Niagara in 1679. On August 7th of that year he sailed for a trip up the lakes, and on the return trip the *Griffin* was lost.

The first sailing vessel on Lake Superior was built at the Soo by the French commandant, Louis Denis, Sieur de la Ronde, in 1734, and was of 25 tons burden. He planned to build an 80 ton ship and develop the copper trade, but the outbreak of the Chippewa-Sioux War, and La Ronde's death soon afterward put an end to these plans.

The first British vessels built on the Great Lakes were a pair of sloops, *Oswego* and *Ontario.* They were launched in 1755 in Lake Ontario.

The first brig-rigged vessel to be built on the Great Lakes was the *London,* in 1756, by the British, on Lake Ontario.

The first American vessel to be built on the Great Lakes was the *Washington,* built at Erie, Pa., in 1797.

15

MEMORIES OF THE LAKES

The first Canadian-built steamboat was the *Frontenac*. The first United States-built Great Lakes steamboat was the *Ontario*. Both were built in 1816. Historians differ as to which was launched first.

The first shipwreck on Lake Michigan was at Chicago, about off what is now 63rd Street. Here the schooner *Hercules* was wrecked and all hands lost. This was in 1818. Indians found the wreck some days later. Bears and wolves had mutilated the bodies of most of the crew.

The first steam vessel on the Upper Lakes was the *Walk-in-the-Water*, of 338 tons, built in 1818 near Buffalo. She was lost in a gale on Lake Erie in 1821. Her engine was salvaged and placed in a second steamer, the *Superior*.

The first steamboat to sail on Lake Michigan did so in 1821 near Green Bay.

The first barge used on the Erie Canal was the *Chief Engineer*, of Rome, New York, in 1826.

The first steamer to reach Sault Ste. Marie was the *Henry Clay* in 1827. Five years earlier the steamer *Superior* with men and materials to build the original Fort Brady, had tried but was stopped at Neebish by low water. The materials were brought up in bateaux and the soldiers marched overland through the woods.

The first coal to reach Cleveland was brought there by Henry Newberry in 1830. Folks were afraid to place it in their fires.

The first shipment by lake to Buffalo was made in the brig *John Kenzie*. It was 3,000 bushels of wheat, and was received in 1836.

GREAT LAKES FIRSTS

The first locomotive used in Chicago was carried there aboard a lakes sailing vessel in 1837.

The first commercial steamer on the Great Lakes to be equipped with a propeller wheel was the *Vandalia,* built in Oswego in 1840. It was also the first steamer to have the engines aft. The propeller was invented by John Ericsson.

The first grain elevator in Buffalo was built in 1842.

The first iron vessel on the Great Lakes was the U. S. Naval Ship *Michigan,* which accidentally launched herself at night at Erie, Pa., in 1844. In 1909 she was renamed *Wolverine.* She was also the first iron vessel in the U. S. Navy. She is still in existence at Erie.

The first steamer on Lake Superior was the *Independence,* built in Chicago in 1845. She brought to the Soo all the equipment to portage herself around the rapids, which took seven weeks. On November 22, 1853 she exploded while just above the Soo Rapids with some loss of life.

First shipment on the Great Lakes of iron ore was made in six barrels on July 7, 1852, in the steamer *Baltimore,* from Marquette, Michigan, to the Soo. The shipment had to be portaged at the Soo, as the canal had not been built. The bill of lading covering this shipment is now owned by the Western Reserve Historical Society.

The first steamboat through the Soo Locks was the side-wheel passenger boat *Illinois* on June 18, 1855. She locked up-bound. Later the same day the steamer *Baltimore* locked down.

The first ore cargo to pass through the Soo Locks was in the brigantine *Columbia,* on August 14, 1855. It was loaded at Marquette for The Cleveland Iron Mining Co.

The first commercial steamer to be constructed of iron was the propeller *Merchant,* of 720 tons, built in 1862 at Buffalo.

The first carferry on the Great Lakes was the *Great Western.* She operated between Detroit and Windsor in 1866. She was built in Glasgow, Scotland, and was brought here in sections and assembled.

The first marine steeple compound steam engine was placed in the steamer *Jay Gould* in 1869.

The first bulk freighter for carrying iron ore was the *R. J. Hackett,* built in 1869, by Harvey Brown in Cleveland, 922 net tons.

The first fore-and-aft compound engine on the lakes was installed in the propeller *Egyptian* in 1873.

The first triple expansion type engines on the lakes were placed in the steamers *Cambria* and *Roumania* in 1887.

A list of the first, or longest vessels on the Great Lakes is interesting. Since 1887, when the first steel vessel came out designed primarily to haul iron ore, there has been no stopping point throughout the years. The list follows:

GREAT LAKES FIRSTS

YEAR	SHIP	LENGTH IN FEET
1887	*Cambria*	300
1888	*Corsica*	312
1889	*Pontiac*	320
1890	*Maryland*	336
1891	*E. C. Pope*	337
1892	*Merida*	380
1895	*Victory*	398
1895	*Zenith City*	407
1896	*Sir Wm. Fairbairn*	445
1898	*Samuel F. B. Morse*	475
1899	*Douglass Houghton*	476
1900	*James J. Hill*	498
1904	*Augustus B. Wolvin*	560
1905	*Henry C. Frick*	569
1906	*J. Pierpont Morgan*	600
1906	*Edward Y. Townsend*	602
1907	*LeGrand S. DeGraff*	605¾
1909	*Shenango*	607
1911	*Col. J. M. Schoonmaker*	617
1925	*Joseph H. Frantz*	618
1927	*L. E. Block*	620¾
1927	*Harry Coulby*	630¾
1942	*Irving S. Olds* (and others)	639¾

The first steel vessel to be lost on the Great Lakes in a gale was the steamer *Western Reserve,* of 1,965 tons. Built in 1890, she foundered in Lake Superior on August 30, 1892, with heavy loss of life.

First cargo of Minnesota's Mesabi Range iron ore to Cleveland was carried in the whaleback barge *102,* with

Capt. E. Peabody. She loaded November 11, 1892 at Superior. The cargo consisted of 2,073 tons of the red mineral. Original bill of lading is now at the Western Reserve Historical Society at Cleveland.

The first quadruple expansion type engines on the Great Lakes were those installed in the steamers *Northwest* and *Unique* in 1894.

The first Hulett ore unloader was installed on the docks in Conneaut in 1899.

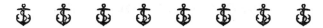

CHAPTER THREE

THE OLD LAKE TRIPLETS

Probably no other ships stand out as clearly in the memories of old timers, whether seamen or travelers on the Great Lakes, than do the passenger steamer triplets, *India, China* and *Japan*. They ran from Buffalo to Duluth, the usual full length trip of the lakes, making calls along the way at Erie, Cleveland, Detroit, Mackinac Island, Marquette and Hancock. These sturdy vessels maintained a highly reliable passenger and freight service for over thirty years and in that time never figured in any serious accident. They were a success from every standpoint, whether of the public, the owners or the crews.

Growing boys in lake ports saw the trim steamers pass, and vowed that some day they would sail aboard those fine ships. Many of them did so, some as passengers, some as crew and some as officers of the boats. The *India, China* and *Japan* are well within the memories of men living today who still enjoy recalling the days of the old craft; days of sustantial growth of a great nation; days when America was forming her future greatness. The days of the lake triplets were truly "the good old days."

The three steamers were built of an early iron, good iron that stood well the test of time, water, wind and weather. At the end of their days the old hulls were practically as good as when launched. It was in a Buffalo shipyard in

1871, the year of the great Chicago fire, that the three boats were launched. Mr. E. T. Evans and his father, Mr. J. C. Evans, of Buffalo, were the men directly responsible for the detailed construction of the triplets. Nine years previously the elder Evans had built an iron ship, the *Merchant*, when such construction was unheard of among shipping men. Today the *Merchant* is recorded as being the first iron ship to sail under the American merchant flag on the Great Lakes. Under the Evans management the triplets eventually came into the Anchor Line fleet, a part of the Pennsylvania Railroad System. They were operated efficiently and were always well kept up and well manned.

The policy of the operators of the line was to name their vessels after a great country or a great city. The triplets were accordingly named *India, China* and *Japan*. A life-size statue of a typical native of each of the countries, hand carved from wood, was mounted atop the pilot house of its corresponding ship. These statues were carefully painted and varnished and were a thing of beauty. At the close of each season they were carefully taken down from their lofty positions and stored ashore, to be redecorated for the coming season.

The head of the Great Lakes was an area of vast wealth and was attracting the attention of men of means. Above ground was the lumber industry in swaddling clothes, while underground copper was king. Iron ore in great quantities came later. The railroads were yet to come through these virgin lands. Through passengers on the triplets traveled to embryo cities of the upper lakes. Later came the immense freight and commerce which they controlled.

THE OLD LAKE TRIPLETS

The triplets were identical in build and until the landsman could read the name on the bow it might be any one of the three. Each of the ships was 210 feet long, 32.6 feet beam and 14 feet depth. They were of the propeller type, with a gross tonnage of 1,239.46 and a net tonnage of 932.02. They made twelve miles per hour.

The three ships were always well painted. Outside, above the main deck they were a spotless white and below that an attractive green. These colors were separated at the main deck by a rich brown fender strake above which was a bright red half-round molding strip. The stack was all red. On the foremast yardarm flew the house flag of the Anchor Line, a white field with a bright red anchor. After each trip the entire ship was washed down, inside and out. The cabins were trimmed in black walnut. All windows and doors had curved tops; there was not a square topped door on a ship.

These fine little vessels had no regular dining room as do the steamers of today. All meals were served in the main cabin, tables running lengthwise of the cabin from the most forward point back to the funnel. Number one table was known as the captain's and that officer usually sat at the head. The galley was on the deck below and the food came up through a dumb-waiter into a pantry on the port side forward. On the opposite side of the cabin was the officers' mess. Directly in the forward part of the cabin was the gentlemen's smoking room and the barber shop. The ladies' cabin was in the after part of the deck and boasted of a piano and easy chairs. When we remember that the day of the triplets was the day of the wash bowl and pitcher ashore, they were equal in all respects to the finest hostelry at any port at which the vessels called.

When these vessels started their runs up and down the Great Lakes their commanders were beset by the perils of navigating along with hundreds of wind-driven schooners. By the time the *India, China* and *Japan* left the lakes scarcely a single sail was to be seen in commercial shipping. Such travel called for the highest type of officers and crew. Many famous men of the lakes have trod the bridges of these ships. Probably the most renowned was Captain Alexander McDougall, designer and inventor of the whale-back type of vessel, so popular in the nineties on the lakes. He sailed the *Japan* in her early days. That three brothers were at one time masters of the triplets is interesting. They were Captain Robert Smith, Captain John Smith and Captain W. W. Smith. A later officer aboard the *Japan* was Captain R. W. England, who is now retired from active sailing but retains a keen interest in affairs of the lakes.

"They were a fine set of boats," remarks Captain England, reminiscently of these bygone ships, "little fellows as steamers of today are measured, but in their days they were tops on the lakes. The service aboard was considered the finest, yet there wasn't a single bathroom on the whole three ships. Each stateroom had what was called running water, but it was supplied by the stewardess who daily filled the little reservoir above the sink faucet from the can of water which she carried about with her on her rounds. Later we had wooden tanks built on the cabin top which really furnished running water to the staterooms. Hot water wasn't thought of.

THE OLD LAKE TRIPLETS

"Each of the ships could accommodate some one hundred and twenty passengers," he continues. "The meals were excellent and the passenger lists were usually filled each trip. At first, of course, the ships had only oil lamps in the cabins, but later a generator was installed in each vessel and we enjoyed the benefits of the early electric light. I well recall that on the *Japan* our generator was run by a belt which in good weather operated perfectly, but when we began to roll the belt would slip off the pulley and instantly the lights all over the ship would go out."

The *Japan* ran on a regular schedule, the captain recalls, and from his memory it was about like this:

TIME-TABLE OF STEAMER JAPAN

About 1896

Leave Buffalo	1 PM	Thursdays
Arrive Erie	9 PM	Thursdays
Leave Erie	11 PM	Thursdays
Arrive Cleveland	8 AM	Fridays
Leave Cleveland	8 PM	Fridays
Arrive Detroit	7 AM	Saturdays
Leave Detroit	Noon	Saturdays
Arrive Mackinac Island	1 PM	Sundays
Leave Mackinac Island	8 PM	Sundays
Arrive Sault Ste. Marie	8 AM	Mondays
Leave Sault Ste. Marie	Noon	Mondays
Arrive Marquette	10 PM	Mondays
Leave Marquette	11 PM	Mondays
Arrive Hancock	10 AM	Tuesdays
Leave Hancock	3 PM	Tuesdays
Arrive Duluth	8 AM	Wednesdays

Leave Duluth	9 PM	Thursdays
Arrive Hancock	Noon	Fridays
Leave Hancock	5 PM	Fridays
Arrive Marquette	11 PM	Fridays
Leave Marquette	10 AM	Saturdays

(Via Grand Island and Pictured Rocks)

Arrive Sault Ste. Marie	8 AM	Sundays
Leave Sault Ste. Marie	9 AM	Sundays
Arrive Mackinac Island	3 PM	Sundays
Leave Mackinac Island	5 PM	Sundays
Arrive Detroit	6 PM	Mondays
Leave Detroit	9 PM	Mondays
Arrive Cleveland	8 AM	Tuesdays
Leave Cleveland	10 AM	Tuesdays
Arrive Erie	9 PM	Tuesdays
Leave Erie	11 PM	Tuesdays
Arrive Buffalo	8 AM	Wednesdays

"This was a good schedule for the Japan and we usually held to it," Captain England relates. "The *India* also ran on the same schedule on alternate weeks. The *China* had a different time-table. We never saw the *China* all season but we met the *India* every Sunday at Mackinac Island for a few hours. It took us two weeks for a complete round trip, but we had plenty of time in port to enable us to have our freight handled. Today the boats make it in one week, but they carry no freight."

The Anchor Line was progressive and always on the outlook for improvement. So it was that in 1901 they brought out the new steamer *Tionesta* at Detroit, and in 1904 the *Juniata* at Cleveland, and in 1910 the *Octorara* at Wyandotte. These new vessels took over the runs of the *India*, *China* and *Japan*. The older ships were sold to Canadian

26

registry. The *India* became the *City of Ottawa,* the *China* became the *City of Montreal* and the *Japan* became the *City of Hamilton.*

Under these new names the triplets still looked alike. They were overhauled and new equipment placed aboard. They entered another lake service, this time their route being from the Canadian ports of Montreal and Toronto to Cleveland, Toledo and Detroit. They were manned by Canadian seamen and for a few years were popular passenger and package freight steamers. Captain John V. Trowell of Toronto was master of the *City of Ottawa* in those years, 1907, 1908 and 1909, and proved to be a popular and dependable skipper.

This Canadian service did not operate over many years. The vessels were again sold and this time they parted company for good. The *City of Hamilton* was eventually converted into a tanker, the *Roy K. Russell,* a barge, and ended her days of usefulness by explosion and fire on Lake Ontario. Her hull was cut into scrap iron at Hamilton in 1935.

The *City of Montreal* had the most lively old age of the triplets. In 1913 she was rebuilt and renamed the *Westerian.* During the next ten years the old ship hauled many a freight cargo. She again changed her name and became the *Sula.* Now she left the Great Lakes and was in the banana trade in the Caribbean Sea and Gulf of Mexico.

Fate returned the *Sula* to the waters of the Great Lakes as in early summer of 1923 she made fast to a dock in Montreal. Here fortune frowned on the fifty-two year old veteran and she was sold at a marshal's sale during that summer. Her new owners gave her back the name *Westerian* and sent her to Quebec where she loaded a general cargo for Orange Bay in Newfoundland. The cargo was delivered but on the return trip and while running light she encountered exceptionally heavy weather in the Straits of Belle Isle.

This storm was too much for the ancient ship and she put back into Saint John's, Newfoundland, and limped mortally creaking to a dock. Her severe beating meant the end for the *Westerian*. She was judged a constructive total loss and was abandoned to the underwriters.

However, there still remained a use for the old hull. Her engines were removed and for about ten years she became a floating salt store in the harbor of Saint John's. Her end came on November 9, 1935 when the remains of the *Westerian*, old and weathered, were towed outside Saint John's Harbor and scuttled in deep water. Thus ended sixty-four years of faithful service of the original steamer *China*.

The *City of Ottawa* was sold back into United States registry and eventually her name *India* was restored, but she was reduced to a barge. As such she changed ownership several times, the last being Mr. C. W. Bryson of Cleveland. He rebuilt the *India* into a fine serviceable craft and put her in the trans-Lake Erie service hauling steel. Thus she served until the start of World War II, when the government took her over and sent her to salt water.

THE OLD LAKE TRIPLETS

The plans of war change swiftly. By the time the old *India* was towed down the Mississippi River, via the Chicago Drainage Canal, and dismantled for reconstruction, the phase of war shipping had so changed that she was abandoned on the edge of Lake Pontchartrain, near New Orleans, Louisiana. Here the last active of the fine old lake triplets now rests awaiting a very dubious future and looking not at all like the trim ship that she was in her heyday when she traded between the rich wonderlands of the upper lakes and the growing commercial ports of the lower lakes.

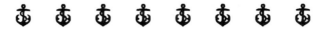

Chapter Four

STEAMBOAT SHORTS

Steamer Chief Justice Waite

Toledo, Ohio, is located a few miles from Lake Erie, upstream on the Maumee River. Some thirty miles eastward of the mouth of the Maumee, in Lake Erie, lies as beautiful a group of islands as can be found anywhere in the world. The most popular of this group is Put-in-Bay, or as the government charts show it, South Bass Island.

Famous millionaires and presidents have vacationed at Put-in-Bay in the nearly one hundred years of its popularity as an island summer resort. In those early years it was a mecca for the old sidewheel steamboats. It naturally follows that Toledo, with its fine harbor, and the nearby resort islands would very early have a steamer connection.

In 1874 the steamer *Chief Justice Waite* made its appearance on this route. She was built at Trenton, Michigan, and was one of the first and finest passenger boats out of Toledo.

An almost sixty year old guide book of the island territory, Nichols' Handy Guide Book, describes the *Chief Justice Waite* in the following complete manner.

"This noble steamer is the property of the Toledo, Lake Erie & Island Steamboat Company. She was built in 1874, is 210 feet long, 48 feet breadth of beam, over all, and 571 tons, drawing 6 feet of water. Her present efficient commander, Capt. Edward McNelly, has had her in charge since the first year she came out. She was built for, and is still engaged in communication between Toledo and the Islands, having frequently conveyed as many as 1,000 to 1,500 persons on a trip, and has been singularly free from the smallest casualties. In point of accommodation she is simply perfect. Capt. McNelly has had a long experience on the lakes and is exceedingly careful and courteous. Mr. L. Goss, as mate, is a thorough sailor and energetic officer. Mr. C. H. Coy, the gentlemanly clerk, is also indefatigable in the exercise of his duties during which he has secured enviable distinction for his affability and gentility. The chief engineer, Mr. A. Weis, is widely experienced and holds a first class certificate, the second engineer being Mr. Culver who is also thoroughly versed in mechanical engineering. The *Chief Justice Waite* is thoroughly equipped from stem to stern and is a delightful vessel on which to enjoy an excursion."

The *Chief Justice Waite* continued to be a popular passenger steamer on Lake Erie during the eighties and made cruises to the various lake ports such as Cleveland, Buffalo, and Detroit. No great news ever broke around the vessel, as she was carefully handled and operated. She was the kind of boat that the public learns to depend upon, and throughout her career she had an enviable record.

Her end did come eventually in Chicago at Grant Park, shortly after the World's Fair in 1893. She had been taken there to operate in the passenger trade during the Fair.

Old and outmoded, she sank and was dismantled.

Recently, in a Florida resort city, a group of men were discussing their various birthplaces. One mentioned that he was born in Cleveland, but that now his birthplace was in Chicago. Unable to understand such a double statement, he was asked for an explanation. It was this. He had been born aboard the steamer *Chief Justice Waite* while the ship was at dock in Cleveland. Since the vessel had later sunk at Chicago, he jokingly claimed his actual birthplace was there at present—in Chicago beneath the waves.

Steamer Pastime

Before the days of the electric interurban car and the automobile, travel followed the waterways. Though the rivers that empty into the Great Lakes are not long, they did offer the early traveler transportation inland from the lakes, and harbor protection. Navigation seldom went over ten miles or so upstream, as shallow water would be encountered. In those days each of these streams had its steamer that hauled passengers and freight between the town at the mouth of the river and as far inland as she could navigate.

Some of these craft took on the appearance of the conventional river steamboat and were not considered able to withstand the seas of the open lakes. They therefore did not venture far from the mouth of their particular river.

Such a boat was the steamer *Pastime* which operated on the Maumee River between Toledo and Perrysburg, Ohio, a distance of about ten miles. Later she operated down river from Toledo to a summer resort then in operation known as Presque Isle, and occasionally into Maumee Bay when weather permitted.

The *Pastime* was 161.8 feet in length and 28.4 feet beam and but 5.4 feet depth. She had large side paddle wheels, each turned by a separate engine operated by steam. She was built on the banks of the Maumee at Toledo in the early nineties, and did a flourishing business until the trolley car with its more frequent service, beat the ship's running time sharply, and so took away the plodding steamer's business.

It was then that the *Pastime* turned to the excursion trade at Presque Isle and to evening rides for its patronage. For several years she enjoyed a good business, but again faster transportation in the form of the automobile caught up with the steamer and left it with too little patronage. Even the resort on Presque Isle folded. It became a coal dock.

The leisurely old *Pastime* also gave up the ghost. According to the old timers who still recall the good times aboard this ship, she was converted into—of all things— a garbage scow. Such is the way of progress.

A travel directory of 1888 describes some of the lake passenger steamers operating in the Lake Erie Islands territory. The quaintness of the descriptions holds a charm worth repeating. It reads as follows.

MEMORIES OF THE LAKES

Steamer Pearl

"The steamer *Pearl* runs daily between Put-in-Bay and Cleveland through the summer months. This beautiful steamer was built in 1875—is 190 x 50 feet over all, 552 tons register, and will carry from 900 to 1,000 passengers in comfort and perfect safety. Her commander, Capt. J. Edwards, is a nautical man of great experience, most attentive, careful, and gentlemanly in deportment, being a special favorite among the passengers on each trip. He ran the first seasons on the *Jay Cooke* and can boast as successful a career as adorns the reputation of any officer on the lakes. The mate, Mr. Gus Plemkie, is largely skilled in navigation, and remarkably steady and prompt to duty. The engine was made by Fletcher & Harris, is an exceedingly fine specimen of mechanism, having a 46 inch cylinder, with 9 foot stroke, and she will steam at fifteen miles an hour, her average trip to the bay running about four and one-half hours to four hours and forty-five minutes, calling at Kelleys Island on her way. Her 1st engineer, Thos. Coford, is a fine machinist, holding a first class certificate, is largely experienced and prompt to duty, being seconded most efficiently by assistant engineer, John Sutcliff, also thoroughly versed in his important duties. The cabins are elegantly furnished, as also the thirty staterooms, which will accommodate from one hundred to one hundred and twenty-five first class passengers; everything about the ship being the "pink" of cleanliness, and a model of system and good order. The indefatigable clerk, Mr. Ebert Clark, is a gentleman whose attentions and courtesies have long established him largely respected among the passengers and the many shippers with whom he transacts business—his promptitude and affability being marked. The boat is amply provided with every modern appliance for an emergency—having the most approved life boats, lifebelts, etc., beside an excellent and ingenious apparatus for the prevention of fire. In short, we may fairly say that the *Pearl* is not surpassed by any boat on the lakes, in any respect. The *Pearl* leaves Cleveland at 8:30 a.m. and arrives at Put-in-Bay at 2 p.m.; leaving Put-in-Bay again at 3:30 p.m.

Steamer Alaska

"The steamer *Alaska* is a most substantially built and rapid steamer, constructed in 1878, and runs through the summer between Detroit, the Islands and Sandusky. She is 361 tons register, and is commanded by Captain A. J. Fox, one of the most skilled nautical officers navigating the lakes. The mate, Mr. John Pender, is also a thoroughly efficient navigator, and the clerk, Mr. A. Clark, is universally appreciated for his promptitude, urbanity, and careful attentions. The engine is a very fine one, kept in the finest condition and presided over by Mr. J. H. Galway as chief engineer with Mr. Julius Holder as assistant engineer, both the latter officials having had a protracted experience. The cabins are admirably fitted and furnished —first class meals and refreshments are served on board, and through the excursion season an efficient string band enhances the pleasure of patrons. This being known as a 'through boat,' there are ample sleeping apartments for 100 to 130 persons, and a table regularly set for 100 to

150, though nearly twice that number have occasionally been dined on board. The *Alaska* leaves Sandusky for the Islands daily (Sunday excepted) at 4 p.m.; arriving in Detroit at 10:30 p.m. Leaves Detroit for Sandusky, calling at the islands, at 8:30 a.m.; arriving in Sandusky at 2:20 p.m. On Sunday leaves Detroit for Put-in-Bay in the morning, returning leaving Put-in-Bay in the afternoon, thus giving passengers a fine view of the islands by daylight.

Steamer City of Sandusky

"The steamer *City of Sandusky* is owned by the Sandusky and Island Steamboat Company. Her captain is Mr. George A. Brown, a gentleman of exceptional nautical skill and experience, being ably supported by Mr. Chas. H. Hubbard, as mate. Mr. W. H. McFall, than whom there is not a more accommodating and gentlemanly representative in the Lake service, is clerk with Messrs. Jacob and Frank Weis, respectively chief and assistant engineers, being mechanics of exceptional skill. The engine, which is a sight to behold for cleanliness, is 750 horse power, her average trips to Put-in-Bay occupying two hours—Kelleys Island being half way. The cabins of this boat are handsomely furnished and carpeted; she has thirty state rooms, capable of accommodating ninety passengers—an excellent piano on board, as also an inviting library of books for the entertainment of patrons. The cook, Mr. George Cooper, is an expert in the culinary department and an experienced sailor. She runs twice daily between Sandusky and Put-in-Bay, not unfrequently performing even heavier duties than this. Her regular summer time card is as follows: Leave Sandusky at 10:00 a.m.; arrive at Put-in-Bay at 12:00 noon; leave Put-in-Bay at 3 p.m.; arrive Sandusky at 5 p.m. Returning, leave Sandusky at 5:45 p.m. arrive at Put-in-Bay at 7:45 p.m.; leave Put-in-Bay at 6 a.m.; arrive at Sandusky at 8:00 a.m., calling at Kelleys Island each way.

Steamer J. K. Secor

"The steamer *J. K. Secor* is a trim little craft running between Put-in-Bay and Port Clinton daily. Her officers are Captain C. Couchaine; mate and clerk, Mr. W. Seafert. She is admirably fitted and an excellent steamer, her time being to leave Put-in-Bay at 6 a.m. and Port Clinton at 3 p.m."

Steamer Post Boy

A booklet entitled "Port Clinton and Environs" published in 1898, tells as follows: "The steamer *Post Boy*, owned by Capt. Jas. E. Spaulding and others of Port Clinton, is the only boat running between Oak Harbor, Port Clinton and Put-in-Bay. This being the shortest distance between any port by boat to the Islands, makes this a most desirable route to take. The distance from Port Clinton is but ten miles, and the time required to make the trip about one hour. The boat is under the management of Capt. Spaulding, one of the chief owners, and a man of many years experience as a lake captain."

♆　♆　♆　♆　♆　♆　♆　♆

CHAPTER FIVE

PIRATES!

Pirates on halcyon Lake Erie? Indeed so! And with
plenty of plot and action behind it all! Lake Erie figured
outstandingly in the War of 1812 when Commodore
Oliver Hazard Perry won his famous naval victory off Put-
In-Bay. It also figured prominently in the Civil War. It
was the last hurdle of the departing fugitive from the
South into the freedom of Canada. It also washed the
shores of the Confederate prison camp on Johnson's Island
in Sandusky Bay.

These two latter facts undoubtedly brought about the
following piratical doings. There were many Southern
sympathizers in Canada. Communication with the Southern Army prisoners, mostly officers, sometimes as many as
three thousand men, was not impossible. So it was that
one John Yates Beall, (sometimes spelled Beale) a lieutenant in the Confederate Navy, at that time on scouting
duty in Canada, planned the piracy and headed the band.
Beall was a college graduate about twenty-one years of
age, and came from a fine and respected family in the
South. His plans were well laid and daring, and he had
enough confidence in them to endeavor to carry them out
himself. Needless to say, his rumored plots caused a great
amount of consternation and uneasiness in the cities and
towns along the lower Great Lakes. Today the story of

PIRATES!

his piratical raid is all but forgotten, but here it is as gleaned from old books and papers still to be found in the vicinity of the action.

The sidewheel steamer *Philo Parsons* left Detroit on her regular run to Sandusky on the morning of September 19, 1864, the third year of the Civil War. Captain S. F. Atwood was in command and Mr. Walter O. Ashley was Ship's Clerk with some forty passengers aboard. On her way down river she stopped at the Canadian town of Sandwich where four rough looking men came aboard taking passage to Sandusky. About twenty miles farther down river at Malden, (now Amherstburg) Ontario, the *Philo Parsons* again made a stop and here around thirty more roughly dressed men boarded the ship also taking passage to Sandusky. No suspicions were aroused, as large numbers of Civil War fugitives were usual travelers to and from Canada in those days. A conspicuous part of their baggage was a large and heavy old style leather covered well roped trunk. This formidable baggage, it was later discovered, contained a young arsenal, having pistols, knives, revolvers, hatchets, and other such menacing weapons.

After leaving Malden the *Philo Parsons* touched at Put-In-Bay and Middle Bass Islands. At the latter Captain Atwood left the boat in charge of the mate, his son-in-law, and went ashore to his home, thereby walking out on the biggest excitement on Lake Erie since Perry's Victory. The *Philo Parsons* continued on her course toward Sandusky, touching at Kelleys Island enroute. Sandusky was to be her next stop and the end of her run. When about three-quarters of the way between Kelleys Island and Cedar Point, and almost within sight of the Johnson's Island Prison Camp, violent things began to happen aboard the usually quiet *Philo Parsons.*

Suddenly the roughly clad men from Sandwich and Malden, at a signal from their leader, Lieutenant Beall, broke open their big trunk and armed themselves. Brandishing their weapons, they took possession of the steamer. The crew were made prisoners and, under point of gun, were forced to navigate the boat as directed by their captors. They entered Sandusky Bay where a better view of Johnson's Island and the Confederate Prison Camp could be had. For some reason not explained they then shut off the engines for a short time; then put the steamer about and returned to Middle Bass Island. Enroute the pirates tossed overboard several tons of pig iron that was consigned to Sandusky, thereby preventing its manufacture into weapons of war. At Middle Bass the *Philo Parsons* was brought to dock and a hurried attempt was made to haul aboard more wood for boiler fuel.

At this point another steamer, the *Island Queen,* came alongside. Her officers were entirely unaware of the plight of the *Philo Parsons.* The *Island Queen* had left Sandusky, bound for Put-In-Bay and Toledo carrying close to one hundred passengers, among whom was a group of unarmed Union soldiers to be mustered out in Toledo.

Beall ordered his men to board the *Island Queen.* Revolvers were brandished, several shots were fired and her crew placed under guard. They, together with all men passengers, were herded aboard the *Philo Parsons* and ordered into the hold. Women and children were to remain in the cabins on the upper deck. Stout resistance was made by Engineer Henry Haines of the *Island Queen* when told to leave his post. He was promptly shot. The bullet grazed his cheek leaving powder burns. Otherwise the raid was conducted in a rather gentlemanly manner.

The passengers were then called upon to pledge themselves to the utmost secrecy for the next twenty-four hours. Agreeing to this, they were put ashore on Middle Bass Island. Captain G. W. Orr of the *Island Queen* together with his wounded engineer and Ship's Clerk William Hamilton, were placed under heavy guard. Beall ordered them to produce the ship's papers which he wanted to send to his headquarters. They could not be found, as the captain's room had already been looted.

The *Island Queen* was then lashed alongside the *Philo Parsons* and Captain Orr was forced to act as pilot. As their progress this way was too slow, the *Island Queen* was ordered cut away and scuttled. A raider went aboard and sawed off her intake water feed pipe. The *Island Queen* quickly filled and settled. By rare good fortune she went down in shoal water at a spot known as Chickanola Reef with much of the ship still showing above water. She was later salvaged.

Freed of her burden, the *Philo Parsons* continued toward Sandusky. About ten o'clock in the evening she again arrived off Sandusky Bay. Lieutenant Beall ordered the ship to lay to and all the raider officers watched landward for a prearranged signal.

In the Bay off Johnson's Island Prison Camp lay the U.

S. Gunboat *Michigan.* To the men aboard the *Philo Parsons* the *Michigan* presented their biggest problem. Their plans called for boarding the gunboat, overpowering her unsuspecting crew, liberating the prisoners on Johnson's Island, and as a final grand flourish raiding the cities along the Great Lakes. A daring plan! But where was the signal?

One of their members had previously been detailed to make the acquaintance of the officers of the *Michigan.* This he had accomplished under the guise of "a man about town." He had been prominent at all the social activities of Sandusky. His part of the plan was to drug the gunboat's officers, leaving the *Michigan* without command. That night he was host at a wine supper given in honor of the officers of the *Michigan* at one of the city's gayest taverns.

All was proceeding well, when in some manner the gunboat's officers became suspicious that they were the victims of a brazen plot. The frustrated Confederate conspirator host was promptly placed under arrest and the banquet guests quickly dispersed. The officers returned to the *Michigan.*

Noting the unusual activity aboard the gunboat and not receiving the expected signal, Lieutenant Beall and his followers realized that their plans had gone astray. They hurriedly brought the *Philo Parsons* about and headed back up the lake toward the mouth of the Detroit River.

The ship's former passengers, previously left on Middle Bass Island, had anxiously scanned the lake for further action during the night. They reported seeing the *Philo Par-*

sons with bright sparks flying from her stack, speed past the island. She was making for the safety of Canada with a full head of steam.

In the Detroit River just above Malden shortly before daybreak they halted the steamer and a number of the raiders went ashore in her small boat. A few miles farther up stream, on Fighting Island, an uninhabited spot of land, the captain of the *Island Queen* and his men were put ashore to shift for themselves. The *Philo Parsons* sailed on a short distance to the Canadian shore where the steamer was abandoned by the pirates and was cast adrift. She was later picked up by a tug and returned to service.

The captain and men left on Fighting Island were shortly rescued by a passing fisherman and were taken to the Michigan mainland where they returned overland to Sandusky to tell of their hair-raising experiences.

The raiders dispersed into Canada after leaving the *Philo Parsons*. Lieutenant Beall was subsequently arrested, tried, and admitted his participation in this and other daring escapades which convicted him as a spy. He was hanged on Governor's Island, New York, on February 24, 1865.

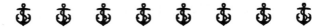

CHAPTER SIX

THE TALE OF THE PEWABIC

Probably the most widely known wreck on the Great Lakes is that of the steamer *Pewabic*. She went to the bottom of Lake Huron four months after the end of the Civil War. Many attempts to salvage the sunken ship's valuable cargo of copper, during the shortage of that material in the days of World War I, brought the old wreck into the headlines and recalled her tragic sinking. Sunken treasure has always had a magnetic appeal, and probably nowhere in the world is there more sunken treasure than lies on the bottom of the Great Lakes. Possibly in some future day much of this untold fortune may be brought to the surface. Millions of dollars of value in ships and cargoes lie within easy reach of the wrecking equipment of today. Possibly the salvage tale of the *Pewabic* may yet be duplicated many times, should future industrial conditions favor such work.

The *Pewabic* was a propeller type wooden vessel in good condition at the time of her sinking. Her crew were regarded as being thoroughly competent. Her captain was George Perry McKay, a young man of twenty-seven years of age. He had been born on a ship, the *Commodore Perry* while it lay in Swan Creek at Toledo, Ohio. All his years had been spent afloat. In 1853, when he was but sixteen years old, he was sailing with his father on the steamer

Independence, which was the first steamer to navigate Lake Superior. When just above the rapids on a regular trip, her boiler exploded causing the loss of the vessel and four lives.

Other officers of the *Pewabic* on this August evening in 1865 were First Mate Cleveland, Steward John Lynch, Clerk Charles Mack, and the lookout was a brother of Captain McKay. She had on board approximately one hundred eighty passengers and a heavy cargo of freight, consisting mostly of copper ingots and ore. This almost pure copper had been placed aboard at Houghton, on the Upper Peninsula of Michigan, and was consigned to Cleveland. Both cargo and passengers were the usual compliment of the ship on its regular trade between the ports of the lower lakes and those of Lake Superior.

It was about nine in the evening. All was well aboard the down-bound *Pewabic* as she steamed along off Thunder Bay in Lake Huron near Alpena, Michigan. A light rain was falling and the breeze was fresh, making the lake a bit choppy. Visibility in spite of the weather was not too bad and the lookout had little difficutly in making out an approaching steamer.

"Steamer ahead, sir, bound this way," he sang out to the officer in the pilot house.

Most of the passengers had already retired to their staterooms, a few still lounged in the eerie oil-lighted cabin and a very few were out on deck.

The upbound ship was shortly made out to be the sister ship of the *Pewabic*, the *Meteor*. It was the usual custom of the vessels when thus meeting to come close together and exchange such effects as newspapers and various messages and mail. The *Meteor* was in charge of Captain Thomas Wilson, a Scotland born young man, who ten years before had come to the Great Lakes and had taken up sailing. Though but twenty-seven years old, he was a well respected and capable skipper.

Oddly, these same two young captains who both survived this ordeal, became big men in the later affairs of the lakes. They continued to follow the lake transportation business for the balance of their long and eventful lives. Captain McKay became the first treasurer of the Lake Carriers' Association as well as superintendent of one of the largest fleets of vessels of the time and an outstanding leader in civic and marine affairs in his home city of Cleveland. He passed away in that city, having attained his four score years. Captain Wilson founded the Wilson Fleet of Great Lakes freight ships in 1873, which continues to the present day. He died in Jerusalem in 1900 while on a vacation. The lives of both shipmasters proved them to have been men of unusual merit.

The two steamers recognized each other while yet a safe distance apart and then proceeded to maneuver to come close. Those on the deck of the *Pewabic* could hear music and see dancers aboard the *Meteor*. What followed will never be definitely known, but in some manner the bow of the *Meteor* crashed into the side of the *Pewabic* cutting a great gaping hole both above and below the water line. Instantly the stricken *Pewabic* started to list as water poured into the opening. Bedlam prevailed aboard the sinking ship. Those dressed and about the ship donned life jackets and shifted for themselves, but those in their state-rooms went down with the vessel. Many of the ones on deck were able to jump to the decks of the *Meteor* and were saved, as that ship, though severly damaged, was able to keep afloat. The two vessels for an instant swung close together and then as the *Pewabic* settled they separated.

In ten minutes time the *Pewabic* had gone down in one hundred eighty feet of water. Her hurricane deck tore loose from the rest of the ship and floated clear. This afforded help for those struggling in the water and several were saved by clambering onto it, later to be taken aboard the *Meteor*. Estimates were that possibly one hundred and twenty-five persons were lost in the disaster.

At daybreak the steamer *Mohawk* came along and the survivors were transferred to that ship and taken to Detroit. The owners of the steamers involved in the col-lision were shocked by the tragedy. It eventually brought about their financial ruin as there was no insurance to cover such a catastrophe. The passengers and owners alike suffered their own losses.

For fifty-two years the cold and clear waters of Lake Huron washed over the wreck of the steamer *Pewabic*. Things ashore changed greatly. Michigan pioneered and prospered. Styles changed. Transportation improved. Large factories began to line the lake shores. Then in 1914 a war broke out in Europe which eventually ensnared the United States. Critical materials became scarce, particu-larly copper. Men began to cast about for copper and someone remembered the cargo of the ill-fated *Pewabic* on the bottom of Lake Huron off Alpena. The price of copper soared until it appeared profitable to attempt to salvage the cargo of the old sunken steamer.

Several attempts were made with varying success. One such, of seven months duration, was by a wrecker who used the sandsucker *Annie Laura* as a salvage boat under the command of the late Captain Charles L. Goodsite. This attempt was reported as being fairly successful.

Another attempt was made under the direction of Captain Fred L. Ermish of Sandusky, Ohio, a professional diver and salvage expert. This was probably the most profitable attempt as a considerable amount of the worthwhile copper cargo was salvaged. Captain Ermish, a man of modest nature, has spent his entire life around water, ships and docks. During his many years of service he is credited with saving the lives of some twenty persons from drowning. He is still active at his chosen work and, during those hectic days at the beginning of World War II, he went to work on overseas dock and defense construction units in the British Isles.

Captain Ermish tells a most interesting narrative of the salvage work done on the old *Pewabic* wreck.

A Toledo concern in 1916 was perfecting a new type of diving suit designed for deeper water than the ordinary suit then in use. Captain Ermish became interested in the effort and was employed to supervise the company's diving activities. The new suit was tested at Traverse City, Michigan, at a depth of 265 feet, but the pressure at this depth was so great that diver was unable to use his arms and legs, as the rubber covered flexible steel tubing that made up those parts of the suit became rigid. Corrections were made and the suit was then offered to the government for use in salvaging the submarine *F-4* which had sunk in Honolulu Harbor. Officials did not accept the suit, as it was considered inadequate. However, this same suit was brought into use in 1917 when salvage operations began on the *Pewabic* wreck and it was found to be very satisfactory.

A copy of the sunken ship's manifest was obtained and, among other things, it called for cargo of 350 tons of copper, salted herring, hides of leather, ships' knees, and a strong box said to contain fifty thousand dollars.

To locate the wreck was the first big task. Several previous attempts had failed. Captain Ermish had orders to try. He arrived in Alpena one morning in May, 1917.

"There was a gale of wind, and so I looked over our equipment," he narrated. "I ordered some changes, and spent the remainder of the day asking many questions from men who had worked on previous attempts to salvage the wreck. I learned that five divers had been drowned in such attempts. I chanced to meet a fine old gentleman, a Captain Persons, who had formerly been employed by the Lighthouse Department at Thunder Bay Island. He furnished me with information which I considered authentic and which later proved to be. He told me that the *Pewabic* lay in a gap, by which he meant a space between Thunder Bay Island and Crooked Island.

"The day after my arrival the weather was fine, and we started out with two boats carrying the equipment to be

49

used in dragging for the wreck. Through my glasses I could see the gap due east about twelve miles from Alpena."

Captain Ermish sailed through the gap, and just beyond began to place eight buoys in a rectangular space. In doing this he carefully followed his instructions from Captain Persons, and also sounded the depth of water under him. He felt certain that the *Pewabic* lay within this rectangular space, provided the old captain had been right in what he had told him.

"We then commenced to drag," he reminisced. "One round trip over the course brought us nothing. On the second trial our cable suddenly became taut, and the more powerful of the two boats commenced to pull the lighter one backwards. I signaled to stop. We lashed the two boats together. I had a seventeen pound special lead with me and 250 feet of line. With this and an oarsman I got into a small boat to see what we had fouled. Considerable current was running this day, and to get our proper depth sounding it was necessary to bring the lead to the top and re-throw it. I worked perhaps three-quarters of an hour before I got a lead on the hull. All at once I noticed that the markings on my line lay slack in my hand. I lifted the lead a trifle off the bottom and as I again dropped it, it went down four more fathoms and I felt certain that we had located the wreck. We pulled in the cable which we had been dragging and found green paint on it. We placed buoys on both ends of the wreck. She appeared to be about 225 feet long but not very wide."

THE TALE OF THE PEWABIC

The best of equipment had been obtained for the operations. The salvage ship was 130 feet long and 40 feet beam. It was equipped with a derrick with a one hundred foot boom capable of lifting one hundred tons. An extra boom with power was also available to handle the diver. When moored at anchor to work she had out two and one-half miles of cable and five anchors handled by power derricks. Her hoisting cables were 500 feet long. Living quarters were below deck. A 220 volt lighting system was also aboard.

Headquarters were established at Alpena. It required four hours to tow the wrecker from there to the site of the wreck. Weather delayed the start, but eventually the men and equipment were on location and ready to begin actual salvage operations.

"We made two dips with our crab," explained Captain Ermish, "which was a large five-fingered affair weighing five tons, and which, when opened, made a circle twelve feet in diameter. The first pass we missed the wreck but brought up something which we could not identify other than that it appeared to be a heavy weight of some sort. In making the second pass we brought up a hand-carved davit and a piece of a covering board. The wind had now increased to such a velocity that we were forced to return to Alpena."

Upon their return to the dock, men familiar with previous attempts at salvaging the *Pewabic*, explained that the heavy weight brought up on their first dip was used by a former wrecker as an anchor to take down their diving bell. These former wreckers had endeavored to salvage the *Pewabic* cargo by the use of the diving bell in their effort seven years before.

"Two divers had descended in this bell which measured eight feet by seven feet," Captain Ermish continued. "One of the glass windows in the bell had cracked, permitting water to enter. Evidently their telephone had gone bad or else the divers would have signaled their tender to raise them to the top. Unfortunately their cable became entangled in the *Pewabic* wreckage and the bell could not be immediately raised. When the cable was at last disentangled by the tender, the bell still could not be raised to the surface, due to its extreme weight, as it had filled with water in the meantime. It was necessary to tow the bell to shore. When it was finally opened the two divers were found dead."

Captain Ermish surmised that all five divers who had previously lost their lives in other attempts had become entangled in the wreck because of strong undertow currents. Consequently he permitted no diving while there was any current. This undoubtedly accounts for the fact that his crew came through without any loss of life.

"I did have one anxious moment though," he mused. "I, myself, was tending one of the divers, and we always maintained at such times a running conversation, usually small talk about anything at all, just so that I knew that everything was as it should be. Abruptly I could no longer get an answer from him. After several attempts to engage him I carefully hoisted him until he was clear of all wreckage. In four seconds I had him clear of the water, he having come from a depth of 185 feet. As I swung him aboard the wrecker his voice came to me in squeaky tones, 'What's the matter with you?' he queried. No voice was ever more welcome for I knew that he was safe. I learned then that he did not know that our communication had been cut off, as he had been talking all the time. A short in the wires was all that was wrong. His voice coming to me as soon as he was out of the water had kept me from breaking the glass in his helmet, the usual procedure in such cases. We did no more diving that day."

The men were able to work on an average of only two and one-half days per week, delays being caused mostly by the weather and currents. No work was attempted on Sunday. On one occasion the outfit had scarcely set to work over the wreck when a gale of wind arose, and they had great difficulty in getting clear of it. It required seven hours of hard battling for the tug to bring them back to Alpena.

"Our big disappointment came," continued Captain Ermish, "upon our fourth trip. The very much coveted ship's strong box was located and brought to the surface. I hastily opened it with bars hoping to find the $50,000 which we had expected would be in gold. Imagine our feelings when we saw that it was paper money, put up in sealed packages. The paper had been so thoroughly saturated that it had become a soggy mass of pulp which resembled somewhat the scales found on the bottom of a well-used tea kettle. A part of some of the bills could be identified but not enough, we believed, to be of any value. Only one five dollar bill remained intact, and we thought it had been covered by a lamp, thus preserving it. This bill, one dollar in gold, two rings—one set with a ruby and the other with sapphires—were all the valuables we received from the finding of that safe."

In locating the safe they brought to the surface the contents of some of the staterooms. Here were grips and trunks containing both men's and women's wearing apparel. In the top of one of the trunks was a lady's silk coat with one sleeve drawn through the other, just as she had placed it there fifty-two years before. Other items included: skirts, with deep handmade lace and embroidery; seven or eight woolen shawls; a woolen hood; a man's suit which had never been worn; twenty-three pairs of leather boots. They carried a box along in which they placed the skulls and heavier bones that were brought up. These were later interred in the cemetery at Alpena.

Up to this time no profit had been made from the venture—it had all been expense. Captain Ermish decided to go after the copper. For several days very little of the precious metal was located. At last it was discovered in the bow of the boat and on the bottom of the lake around the bow. This proved that the *Pewabic* had gone down bow first. It indicated that at one time she must have been perpendicular enough to allow the heavy copper to slide off her deck, tearing away her forward bulwarks. The wreckers had expected to find the copper in her hold but, upon breaking through her main deck with their huge crab, they found only leather, barrels of salted fish, and ship's knees. Had the entire cargo of copper been in her hold it would have been much easier to salvage. One day they brought up twelve thousand dollars worth of the metal in two hours. They had to stop when a gale sprang up and they were forced to retire to shelter.

When the operations finally ceased only fifty-five of the reported 350 tons of copper had been retrieved, but this was enough to pay all expenses and leave a small profit. They received five hundred dollars per ton for their salvaged copper. Two particularly large pieces were recovered, one weighing four tons and the other five tons. This latter was said to have been the largest piece known to have been mined up to that time.

The various salvaged articles attracted wide attention in and around Alpena. All the items were assembled in a vacant store and made into an exhibit for the benefit of the Red Cross. The first person to view them was a woman eighty-two years old. She signed her name on the register with a pencil salvaged from the *Pewabic*. She said that she had lost relatives in the sinking and had come two miles on foot to see the display. The Detroit & Cleveland steamers, then calling regularly at Alpena, laid over in this port long enough for their passengers to view the display.

"It was quite a display, too," remarked Captain Ermish. "There were, of course, copper in its various forms, lead pencils, parts of musical instruments, the captain's binoculars, clothing of all kinds, shoes, rubbers, buttons, tintypes in a perfect state of preservation, books which could still be read, dishes, knives and forks bearing the name *Pewabic*. In the food line there were canned sardines, salted fish in barrels, mixed pickles and a considerable amount of sarsaparilla pop. Members of our crew drank

55

some of that ancient beverage and ate some of the sardines, and thought them not so bad. There was money in different denominations, both in gold and silver; purses with men's names on them; horses hoofs and some bones of the two horses that went down with the ship, even their halters. There were human bones of all sorts and some human flesh. There were watches, jade jewelry, hairnets with the rubber still intact, ship's knees, and of course the disappointing strong box which had contained the paper money.

"We also had timbers from the starboard side of the *Pewabic* which had been smashed in the collision; parts of the ship's machinery; her water hose which was made of leather; her bilge pump which was made of wood; tackle blocks carrying the name of the ship; some of her fenders which were made in three pieces and held together by wooden pins; some pieces of coal which she carried for her own use (not as cargo) and which were as light as feathers; cordwood used for fuel; and a large English razor made by Wade & Butcher. I was shaved with this razor later in an Alpena barber shop. We brought up the *Pewabic's* huge anchor, too, and we used it to anchor our own equipment for a while, but we lost it among the wreckage of the boat it had served, so there we let it remain."

And so rests on the bottom of Lake Huron the battered and scattered wreckage of the *Pewabic,* the old steamer of Civil War days. But what of the *Meteor,* the other vessel in that fateful collision? Fortune smiled upon her after her one ugly thrust into the *Pewabic.* Records show that she was repaired and found a useful and profitable existence in Great Lakes commerce. Eventually she became obsolete. A fire ravaged her. She was cut down into a tow barge. Her name was changed to *Nelson Bloom*. She again sailed the lakes, hauling bulk cargo. This continued throughout World War I, truly a remarkable record of wooden boat usefullness! Eventually she went the way of all such ships, rotted and abandoned.

Chapter Seven

THE BONES OF THE PORCUPINE

Just a bundle of old bones! Many a fine ship has ended her days in that fashion. But somehow the old bones of the *Porcupine* seemed different. Maybe it was because they were not being washed by the waves. Instead they lay carefully stacked, miles from any water, in a storeroom of The Western Reserve Historical Society in Cleveland, awaiting the time when they would be put on exhibition. Nearby stood two boxes of wrought iron spikes and other small pieces of the old vessel. Around those old relics is woven a history, and marine tales are told that stir the blood.

The sloop of which these timbers were a part played an active part in a major naval engagement. Her commander later was killed ashore in a duel. Then followed many years of commercial sailing. Later came abandonment, sinking, years underwater, raising, rotting on shore; then recognition and salvaging, with the height reached when she was placed on display for thousands to view. Now she is temporarily resting until a permanent display is arranged. A truly exciting and worth while career!

One hundred and thirty odd years ago these dirty old timbers were great growing trees of oak, part of the vast forests which lined the shores of Lake Erie. War was in

58

the air. To Erie, on the southern shore of the lake by that name, came sailors to fight. They needed ships. Every war needs ships. So it was that these great trees fell to the woodsman's axe. The shipbuilder took them, and with his tools he fashioned them into ships that would float upon the water, and bear guns and cannons, and brave men to fire them. A leader came to these fighters. He was Oliver Hazard Perry, then a young man of twenty-eight years. He held the rank of lieutenant in the infant United States Navy.

These particular timber bones, then strong new wood, found themselves a part of the sloop *Porcupine*. This vessel was almost the smallest of Perry's fleet of nine boats. She carried only one gun. However, big or small in size, she played an interesting part in the Battle of Lake Erie, fought on September 10, 1813. Any American history will tell of the famous battle in which Perry's men outfought the British, under Barclay, and of the turn of the war at this point which shortly resulted in an American victory and consequent peace.

Those stout timbers that made up the *Porcupine* had been shelled at close range by the British in desperate combat. British bullets were firmly imbedded in them, to stay there for many years. American blood ran thick over her tiny deck, and the smoke of battle filled her hold.

When man at last laid down his weapons, and peace came to the lakes, the *Porcupine* was still a sound vessel. A commerce was being born on this great inland waterway that was destined to be second to none. The *Porcupine,* minus her one gun, entered this growing commerce as a freight boat. She was taken to Lake Michigan and was sailed out of Grand Haven. Lumber, fresh cut and pleasant to smell, was piled high on her deck, and salt was carried in her hold. Years passed, young men grew into old men, and still they watched the *Porcupine* sail out upon the bosom of Lake Michigan with heavy cargo.

After some sixty years in such trade the timbers of the *Porcupine* began to show the ravages of time. She became unseaworthy, and man would no longer trust himself aboard her. Daring fishermen took some chances on short cruises with her, but they soon abandoned the aging craft. She was hauled away from big Lake Michigan, up the Grand River, and into little Spring Lake.

Here the valiant sloop sank along the shore, and trout and other lake fish found haven in her hold. For almost a quarter of a century winter ice and summer waves succeeded each other in surrounding this forgotten little sloop. Forgotten? Not altogether! There were a few men who still remembered and cared.

One such man busied himself with the gigantic task of hauling the derelict out of the water and up on solid, dry ground. Slowly, and with much hard work, the vessel was brought out of the water which had been her element for so long. She was laid upon the sod under some apple trees, her tall masts being long since gone. Many times the bones of the old *Porcupine* saw the lovely blossoms come on the apple orchard, and the fruit ripen into luscious apples. Strong fall winds filled the crannies of her hull with leaves, and winter storms whisked falling snow over the packed leaves. The old bones weakened. Rot set in.

THE BONES OF THE PORCUPINE

Thus was nature reducing the *Porcupine* to the inevitable dust.

Here the story might have ended had not word come to the quiet orchard-lined shores of Spring Lake that a great celebration was being arranged to honor the one hundredth anniversary of the Battle of Lake Erie, and the enduring peace which followed between the two great neighboring nations on the Great Lakes.

Men recalled the whereabouts of the little sloop *Porcupine* that had played such an active part in the battle. They started to bring her into light. The parts that were left of her—only her stout keel, some ribs, and very little planking—were carefully loaded and shipped to the busy scenes of the Perry Victory Centennial Celebration.

Here the old bones that had endured so much for so long were placed under bright display lights, where the admiring public passed before the tired remains of the old vessel and recalled the long and eventful career of the little *Porcupine*.

The giant celebration over, janitors hauled away the remaining timbers of the old boat. This time they went into the lowest basement of the City Hall in Cleveland, to remain dark and forgotten, while life swirled on above them. For about a score of years they rested there until someone again remembered.

A place for everything and everything in its place! So it was that in the halls of the Western Reserve Historical Society a proper place was found for the old bones of the little sloop *Porcupine,* now reduced to only a bundle and a couple of boxes, but still great in memories. Here, fortunately, someone cares for the ship that is now "just a bundle of old bones."

⚓ ⚓ ⚓ ⚓ ⚓ ⚓ ⚓ ⚓

CHAPTER EIGHT

HIGH SPOTS IN GEORGIAN BAY

Georgian Bay is a great body of fresh water. While far from being the most traveled, it has probably the most rustic shores of any of the Great Lakes. Charts show it as a part of Lake Huron. However, measured in square miles, Georgian Bay compares well with the better known Lake Ontario. The former has 7,000 square miles of surface, including the North Channel, while the latter has 7,330 square miles. It is located entirely within the Province of Ontario, Canada. A bit off the beaten commercial track of the Great Lakes, Georgian Bay is truly the nature lovers' paradise. Dense woods and deep rivers abound. Fine Canadian towns are also on its shore line. Some are busy and thriving and forging ahead, while others are still in a quiet state of lethargy, as unkempt native Indians wander about the unpaved streets and into the few backwoods general stores. A charming quaintness exists in such villages. During the summer months the few tourists who find their way into them are well rewarded in their search for the singular or unique.

The first white men to cast their eyes upon the waters of the Great Lakes stood on the shores of what is now Georgian Bay. This was in 1615 when Champlain and Brule and their bands of hardy explorers floated down the beautiful French River to where it emptied into the great body of water now known as Georgian Bay. They had come laboriously upstream on the Ottawa River from where it joins the Saint Lawrence near Montreal. Pushing westward they had portaged their equipment when necessary, had crossed the wilderness water of Lake Nipissing and then found the French River which they descended to its mouth, there to make their great discovery.

Numerically impressive, Georgian Bay boasts justly of its Thirty Thousand Islands. Here nature has been truly lavish in her bestowal of water-surrounded land. The largest island in fresh water in the world and likely the tiniest island, only large enough for a man to stand upon, are found in Georgian Bay.

Manitoulin Island lays claim as the largest island with its 1,073 square miles. It separates the Bay from Lake Huron. Good harbors abound. Its surface is dotted with nearly one hundred clear lakes. The unique town of Little Current is the island's largest trading center. Here Whites and Indians mingle on the few quaint streets and in the shops as they procure their supplies.

The majority of the islands comprising the group known as the Thirty Thousands Islands are rugged wooded spots on solid stone bases. Some of the stone underlying the land rise straight and broad from the cold waters of the Bay, while some slope gently into the rippling surface of the water. To the northward on the mainland lie the weather-beaten rounded ridges of the ages-old Laurentian Mountains. The Georgian Bay district is a grand challenge for the traveler looking for something different.

HIGH SPOTS IN GEORGIAN BAY

For as many years as water travel has been known on the lakes, Georgian Bay has been navigated. It still rightfully boasts of some of the finest lake liners afloat. Hundreds of tales of ships that have plied the waters of Georgian Bay are told by the old-timers in the towns and cities along the shore line. One hears them spun in Owen Sound, Collingwood, Midland, Port McNicoll, Parry Sound, and by the hardy fishermen in rocky Killarney and in Tobermory, way out at the tip of the Saugeen Peninsula. At Byng Inlet and Key Harbor, former extensive lumber shipping ports on the north shore, one still hears the echoes of the now extinct lumber "hookers" and of their hardy crews and the equally burly lumberjacks.

Almost all historically minded communities along the Great Lakes can point with pride to an ancient shipwreck and practically prove that there lie the bones of the *Griffin*, the first sailing craft ever to sail the Great Lakes. This famous old vessel carried La Salle and his party up the lakes in 1679, and was lost completely on her return down the lakes in charge of a few trusted men of the party.

Manitoulin Island is no exception to this claim. The remains of a shipwreck lie on the westerly coast of the island near Mississagi Lighthouse. Statement is made that scientific analysis of the metal in this wreck points to the fact that it may be La Salle's *Griffin*. It could be. Neither historian nor scientist has yet proven where the *Griffin* is hidden, if hidden she is. One man's guess today is as good as another's.

Probably the most repeated Georgian Bay tale is that of the old steamer *Waubuno*. Popular too are the stories cf the *Asia* and the *Mary Ward*. There are dozens of such anecdotes from the early windjammers up to the wrecks of modern freighters. It would require volumes to tell them all.

The wreck of the *Waubuno* tale has that touch of mystery that makes it most interesting. A bride's dream of shipwreck that came true and found her and her husband victims, adds color to the story. No survivors to explain what had happened deepens the mystery. No bodies were ever found to add their mute evidence. A wrecked hull which floated upside down into a safe harbor months later brings the mystery to its climax.

The fourteen year old sidewheel steamer *Waubuno* stretched her hundred and fifty feet of length against a dock in Collingwood. She was heavily loaded with various kinds of merchandise and supplies. A few passengers bound for Parry Sound, the steamer's destination, restlessly awaited the boat's departure. Captain George Burkett paced back and forth in his tiny pilot house listening to the howling gale outside. Snow had swirled around the little structure and had whitened the windows until they were quite useless.

Maybe the bride's dream bothered him. She had told it all too convincingly. Among his passengers who had come aboard the night previous were a young doctor and his attractive bride, bound for the north country where the husband intended to set up his practice. An unusually severe early winter storm—it was then late in November, 1879—had delayed the sailing of the *Waubuno*, and passengers and crew were beginning to get irked. The bride told of dreaming of the shipwreck of the *Waubuno,* and of seeing in her dream the tragic drowning of her husband and all on board. The next morning she had implored the young doctor to leave the ship and to proceed overland to their destination. He attempted to quiet her anxiety, explaining that it was only a foolish fancy, born of a dream.

The following day as the vessel still awaited better sailing weather, the worried bride told other passengers of her apprehensions. Soon the word swept through the whole ship's company, passengers and crew alike. Now it was the second night. The bride's dream story had even gone ashore and through the town.

About four in the morning the snow and gale had abated somewhat. Captain Burkett, poo-pooing the dream tale, ordered his crew to prepare to sail. The *Waubuno* cleared the harbor. She was last seen by the lighthouse keeper on Christian Island as she passed his station.

She never arrived in Parry Sound. Search was made over her course and bits of wreckage were found, but never a sign of the bodies of any of her passengers or crew. Twenty-four persons had vanished. Lumbermen working near Moon River told of hearing a ship's whistle sounding constantly but due to the blinding snow which had resumed its heavy fall, they were unable to locate any vessel.

Late the following March, an Indian wandered into Parry Sound and told of seeing a big boat bottom-up near Moose Point and the Haystacks. Subsequent investigation proved that the Indian was right. It was the overturned hull of the ill-fated *Waubuno*. There was nothing to indicate what had happened to the steamer. Her upper cabins had broken off the hull as she lay upside down. The hull was intact with no tell-tale scars. For many years the hull of the *Waubuno* lay grounded in the bay near Moose Point. It may still be there. The pretty bride's dream had come true!

The story of the *Mary Ward* is less spectacular and without mystery, but it carries the elements of the hazards of early navigation; mistaken lights on the shore; inadequate life saving equipment and the ever present error of too hasty human judgment.

Seven years earlier than the *Waubuno* disaster, to the very day, November 22, 1872, the little propeller *Mary Ward* sailed from Sarnia bound for Owen Sound and Collingwood loaded with salt, coal oil, various kinds of merchandise and a number of passengers. She stopped at Tobermory for wood for her boilers and a few more passengers. On the morning of November 24th she reached Owen Sound where still more passengers boarded the little steamer. She sailed that afternoon for her destination, Collingwood.

That was a beautiful Sunday afternoon. Just the faintest south breeze rippled the clear waters of Georgian Bay. Collingwood lay but six sailing hours distant. Such a day was what the lake mariners termed a "weather breeder"— it usually breeds bad weather. So it did. Most of the trip was completed when late in the afternoon a fresh breeze sprang up and suddenly shifted into the northwest. Sunday night came on quickly and was unusually black. What was believed by the ship's officers to be the Nottawasaga Lighthouse was located and the course was laid based on that light.

A few minutes before nine the real Nottawasaga Light was located, but too late. The *Mary Ward* crashed herself onto a smooth shelving hard shoal some three miles off shore. Her officers assured the passengers that there was no danger—the ship would be released by tugs from Collingwood in the morning. The purser and a man passenger put off in a small boat to seek aid. They arrived safely at a dock in Collingwood early Monday morning, just ahead of a howling gale that was destined to wreak vengeance on the helpless stranded little steamer.

At two that afternoon the tug *Mary Ann* left Collingwood to aid the *Mary Ward*. The storm was then at its peak and huge waves were beating against the steamer with such violence that they threatened to pound her to pieces. The captain and a few of the men passengers had previously left the steamer in another small boat and had headed for the Nottawasaga Lighthouse to seek further help, fearing that something had happened to prevent the purser from reaching Collingwood.

Upon the arrival of the tug *Mary Ann* at the stricken vessel it was evident that it would be impossible to get a line aboard the wreck, so great were the seas. The tug reluctantly returned to her dock. Believing that their ship would soon break up, eight men, some belonging to the crew and some passengers, decided to make a break for the shore in the remaining small boat. It was a foolhardy experiment. They had scarcely left the steamer when their frail craft capsized and all were lost. This constituted the only loss of life in the wreck.

By evening the gale blew itself out. Later three husky fishing boats came alongside and rescued those persons who had remained aboard. The *Mary Ward* was a total loss. The ledge on which the little steamer had wrecked herself was thereafter known as the *Mary Ward* Shoal. Today, seventy-four years after the famous wreck, the Mary Ward Shoal stands well out of the water, a rocky ridge, left there by nature's receding waters. On calm days the remains of the *Mary Ward* can still be seen lying deep in the water on the rocky bottom, parts of her hull, her propeller, her engines, and her boiler.

While the folks in the Georgian Bay Country were still talking of the mysterious disappearance of the *Waubuno*, another ship with a larger passenger list would have as mysteriously disappeared had it not been for the good fortune of a young lady and a young man. The fates decreed that those two should live to come ashore and explain what had happened to their ship.

The wooden Canadian propeller *Asia* of 350 tons burden lay at her wharf in Collingwood on Wednesday, September 13, 1882, taking aboard a merchandise cargo and a goodly list of passengers bound for French River and Sault Ste. Marie. Persons in those days did their traveling on the water whenever possible. The lake ships almost always carried full passengers lists, except where competition placed too many vessels on a particular run. The Georgian Bay ports drew a satisfactory volume of trade both in freight and passengers.

The nine year old *Asia* completed her loading in Collingwood and sailed early in the morning for Owen Sound where she took aboard more passengers and freight. When she left there she carried one hundred twenty-five persons, both passengers and crew, and a heavy package freight cargo.

As the *Asia* put the lights of Owen Sound behind her, Captain John Savage noted with some concern the rising wind which was kicking up a bit of a sea. But time, even in those days, was precious, and captains did not like to lose any of it lying alongside a dock when they could be going places out on the broad waters. So the *Asia* plowed on through the rising seas that night.

Very early the next morning a stop was made for fuel. The *Asia* fueled with wood from the nearby forests. The supplying of such steamboat fuel formed no small industry along the shores of all the Great Lakes.

That day the wind continued and the seas mounted. The *Asia* rolled and pitched in spite of her heavy load as she made her way northward up Georgian Bay. Many of her passengers were in their bunks too ill to be about the vessel. The cargo began to slide about her decks, first to one side and then to the other. It was impossible for the crew to keep their ship on an even keel. This condition grew steadily worse until about noon, just as Lonely Island dimly appeared in the distance ahead. Lonely Island was a comforting sight to Captain Savage. Here at least would be partial safety. Even though it was a comparatively small piece of land it was solid and unsinkable. But the *Asia* never made Lonely Island. She foundered within sight of it.

Eighteen persons were able to leave the *Asia* in a life boat and head for land. Luck was against most of them. The seas were running too high for the small boat, and several times it capsized throwing its occupants into the raging waters. Only two lived through that ordeal to step onto dry land again. They were Miss Christena Ann Morrison and seventeen year old Duncan A. Tinkiss. Young Tinkiss and Miss Morrison had found themselves in opposite ends of the life boat. As the boat would roll over and spill out its human cargo into the water each of them would grasp the very end of the small boat, hang on and then clamber back in it again when it quieted. One hundred twenty-three less fortunate souls perished in the foundering of the *Asia*. Tinkiss and Miss Morrison were later found by an Indian who loaded them into his frail craft and brought them into Parry Sound three days after their steamer had gone to the bottom of Georgian Bay. Thus was the disappearance of the *Asia* made known.

Today's men of the Georgian Bay district tell some stories of the more modern vessels that have encountered difficulty in these waters. Their tales are less colorful but equally exciting. They mention the stranding of the big freighter *Western Star* on Robertson's Rock, a dangerous menace to any shipping that happens its way. Only a very little water covers this rock that rears itself from the bottom of the bay and the luckless *Western Star* chanced to pile herself onto it. The freighter was later salvaged by the wrecker *Favorite* in a major salvage feat, and returned to do many years of valuable service on the lakes.

Another comparatively recent wreck story of Georgian Bay is that of the freighter *North Wind*. Twenty minutes after she had cast off her lines from a dock at Parry Sound she lay on the bottom of the bay. In navigating the tortuous channel the wheelsman evidently misunderstood an order of the captain's and put the wheel the wrong way. The result was a grinding crash as the bow of the steamer struck a submerged rock and quickly sank in deep water. All on board were saved although they lost whatever belongings they had on the ship.

Another popular tale is that of the little passenger boat *Hibou*. This twenty-nine year old vessel, on the morning of November 21, 1936, sank beneath the waves in Owen Sound Bay in ninety feet of water when about two miles from her dock. With the *Hibou* went her cargo of flour and general merchandise. Seven members of her crew perished.

The *Hibou* lay upright on the bottom between two large boulders while six successive winters of heavy ice froze and thawed over her. Then came Captain J. T. Reid of Sarnia with wrecking equipment and successfully raised the *Hibou* from the depths to float again upon the Great Lakes waters. A really remarkable salvage feat!

Truly, Georgian Bay has the longest history of man's sailing activities upon the Great Lakes.

MEMORIES OF THE LAKES

And so go the tales of shipwreck and disaster of the early and modern days of navigation on the usually tranquil waters of Georgian Bay. Nothing is mentioned of the thousands of trips made in safety with never-to-be-forgotten pleasure over these charming waters. Only the grim tales remain to be told again and again.

Chapter Nine

THE MILAN CANAL

From the reputed "greatest grain port in the world" to a quiet little inland town, many miles from a ship's dock, is the very interesting tale of modest little Milan, Ohio,

Here indeed is a town rich in memories. Thomas Alva Edison brought everlasting fame to it by being born there on February 11th, 1847, in a little brick dwelling which is still standing. His birth occurred at the time that Milan was a famous grain shipping port.

Early settlers had previously come to the spot where now stands Milan and had built a thriving village. It was in the heart of what was known as "The Firelands," so named because the State of Connecticut offered its citizens restitution there for the burning of their farms and homes by the British during the Revolutionary War. Hardy pioneers in coonskin fought their way through the forest primeval from Connecticut to the Firelands of the Western Reserve. As the forests were cut down to make way for grain fields this section became very productive. Surpluses in grain grew. Markets had to be found. Transportation was the problem. Railroads were still to come, born of this same necessity.

Milan's citizens thought out a sound plan. The Huron River, deep enough for the lake schooners of the day, was nearby, wandering its way into Lake Erie. By this route the surplus grain of the Milan countryside could be shipped to the growing markets in the ports that were springing into existence along the shores of the Great Lakes.

So Milan raised funds for a canal to bring the waters of the Huron River to its door. Its first estimate of $5,800 proved to be much too low, but work started in 1833. Six years later the canal was completed at a cost of $23,392. It was three miles long and contained two locks.

On July 4, 1839, amid a great celebration, the lake schooner *Kewaunee* tied up at the wharf in Milan. Farmers for one hundred and fifty miles to the southward drove their great lumbering covered wagons loaded with grain to the storage elevators that had sprung up on the canal banks at Milan. They returned home loaded with supplies. Trade had rushed into Milan with the arrival of the *Kewaunee.* Hundreds of such vessels loaded grain at Milan, navigated the three mile canal into the Huron River, and thence into Lake Erie and the Great Lakes. They brought supplies into Milan from the outer world. On an average of fifteen vessels a week entered and cleared the odd port of Milan.

Other industries came into being along the banks of the Milan Canal and the Huron River. Shipbuilding was outstanding. Fine timber stood close at hand. Valentine Fries built a large plant opposite the entrance of the canal on the river. Here were turned out several of the finest craft to sail the waters of the Great Lakes. Outstanding was the three-masted schooner *Golden Age,* built in 1883, with a carrying capacity of about three thousand six hundred tons. This sturdy vessel plied her trade on the lakes for forty-one years. Unlike most of her type, she was not lost in storm, but faithfully delivered her last cargo to the dock. Eventually she was taken to South Bass Island in Lake Erie and sunk near shore as a breakwater protection. The *Golden Age* was one of the best and largest boats of her day.

Fries also constructed at his yard the three thousand two hundred ton schooner *Charles Foster*, in 1877. Probably the most outstanding effort of the Fries yard was the building of the steamer *William Edwards*, in 1879, of two thousand five hundred tons cargo capacity. This ship was very popular from Duluth to Buffalo for many years. The *William Edwards* towed the *Golden Age* for many seasons. Finally, aged and worn out, the *William Edwards* near the outset of World War I, was sent to Europe with a cargo of timbers for the Allies. She never returned to her native fresh water, as she was lost enroute to Europe.

Other craft to be built by Fries included the *Marion W. Page*, 749 tons, in 1876, *Atmosphere*, 276 tons; *Amaranth*, 272 tons. From other shipyards along the Milan Canal and Huron River came the *Cuba*, of 190 tons; the *Eunice*, of 234 tons; and the *Surprise*, of 222 tons, all built in 1856. The *Timothy Baker*, 719 tons, was launched in 1857. The *Day Spring*, *Jesse L. Boyce*, *H. S. Walbridge*, *Jura* and *William Shupe* came out in 1862. The schooners *Samuel J. Holley*, *A. J. Mowry*, *Myrtle*, *Mystic*, *Exile*, *M. Stalker*, *Winona*, *Monsoon*, *Pilgrim*, *Hyphen*, *Kate Norton*, and the *Idaho*, all slid down the ways from these shipyards.

77

MEMORIES OF THE LAKES

Most of the Milan built boats had long and successful careers. However, one, the *Kate Norton,* had a very short existence and a tragic ending. Proclaimed as one of the smartest vessels to be launched in the late 1850's, she was outfitted for the Great Lakes trade and left Milan late one Friday afternoon in the spring, with her white sails bellying to the breeze, and her fresh paint and varnish work glistening in the setting sun. Thus did the schooner *Kate Norton,* under the command of Captain Homer Beardsley, clear the harbor of Huron and enter Lake Erie. She sailed away into Eternity. Her first night on the "Great Waters" was also her last, a rare record for a sturdy ship. A storm came up during the night and when daylight came the *Kate Norton* was gone. None of her crew lived to tell her story. Another of those ill-fated craft to add her name to the long list of ships that had "sailed away."

Old-timers tell the *Kate Norton* story with the admonition that a new vessel should never start out on a Friday. Captain Beardsley had defied this old superstition when he cast off the schooner's lines at Milan on that fateful Friday.

To the 350 ton schooner, *Idaho,* goes the record of being the last vessel to enter the old Milan Canal. Her story is entwined with the fall of Milan as a grain port, or even a port.

The year 1847, in which Thomas Alva Edison was born, found Milan at its peak in the shipment of grain. Records indicate that that year this odd Ohio port shipped grain on

78

THE MILAN CANAL

a par with Odessa, Russia, at that time a world famous grain shipping center. However, the following year Milan's shipments of grain began to decline. Competition was beginning to out-date her canal. The business of transportation by rail was commencing in earnest in the lake country. Each year the figures showed less and less grain leaving Milan. The loaded schooners heading lakeward became fewer, and finally shipments by water ceased completely. Only the shipbuilding industry continued. It too slowed to an eventual stop. Folks left Milan for more prosperous places.

But to go back to the schooner *Idaho* and the part she played in the ending of the Milan Canal. The grain trade was well on the decline when the *Idaho* was launched in 1863. Her length was one hundred thirty-five feet.

The *Idaho* enjoyed profitable and good sailing up and down the Great Lakes in the coal and general merchandise trade, along with an occasional grain cargo. The year 1873, exactly ten years after her launching, found the *Idaho* heading upstream in the Huron River toward the Milan Canal for overhauling. Competition was squeezing the profit out of the operation of the little *Idaho*. Rates were falling and larger ships were taking the cargoes.

Upon reaching the Milan Canal, the *Idaho* tied up to the slowly disintegrating wharf, paid off her crew, and rested, the idea of overhauling being abandoned. The water in the canal was then of questionable depth for the schooner and it was thought best to lay her up where she would have better exit to the lake. So she was laid up temporarily within the lock of the canal where it entered the Huron River, near Abbott's Bridge. This spot proved to be her final resting place.

Each year found the *Idaho* more and more out-moded, and in worse state of repair. No more vessels cared to navigate the once busy canal, and the *Idaho* gradually fell into decay, along with the canal locks, wharfs, elevators, and all that had once made Milan a thriving port. The canal dried up. Milan was no longer a port, its connection with deep water was gone.

Eventually the remaining industry, mostly wooden ship-building that had flourished along the Huron River, also died. The sounds of the shipbuilder's adze, hammer, and saw, were quieted, and the weeds grew upon the well trodden soil where once the schooners were built. Navigation quit the Huron River, except near its entrance to Lake Erie. Land transportation had brought its products nearer to deep water more economically than the vessels could be brought into the land. This fact was far reaching in its effect, even resulting in the eventual decay of the great system of Ohio canals that stretched from the Ohio River to Lake Erie.

If one today were to locate the spot near Abbott's Bridge where the Milan Canal entered the Huron River, and were he to grub around in the now tall growth on the exact site, he might still find the decaying bones of the old *Idaho* where she has rested for nearly four score years, buried there by the hand of nature.

Along with the *Idaho* are buried the memories of the once thriving grain port of Milan, Ohio, now many miles from any possible commercial navigation.

PICTORIAL
SECTION

CHAPTER TEN

United States Gunboat *Michigan*. Name changed in 1905 to *Wolverine*. Launched at Erie in 1843. Her iron hull, considered the oldest in the world, lies not far from where it was launched. Efforts are being made to save it from the scrap pile.—*From a painting by Charles R. Patterson. Photo copy gift of Mr. Herbert R. Spencer.*

MEMORIES OF THE LAKES
TOLD IN PICTURES

Each of the following views is itself a pictorial memory of the Great Lakes. It is believed that all the ships shown have disappeared from the lakes, unless so mentioned. Obviously, the entire collection is the result of the efforts of many people. The author has gathered together the views from greatly varied sources. Where origin of the photograph is known, it is so mentioned, also the collection from which it is presented or loaned.

81

FOR LAKE SUPERIOR.

The New & Splendid   *Side-wheel Steamer,*

NORTHWEST,

C. E. KIRTLAND, Commander,

Will leave BRADY & CO.'S dock, foot of Woodward Ave., Detroit, **Every Tuesday**, for SAUT ST. MARIE, MARQUETTE, HOUGHTON, and HANCOCK, touching at Sarnia and Port Huron, every TUESDAY EVENING at 10 o'clock.

For Freight or Passage apply to
BRADY & CO., foot of Woodward Avenue, Detroit·

CHARLES H. BALDWIN, Passenger Agent.

1868.   SEASON ARRANGEMENTS.   1868.

Detroit, Saginaw, and Lake Huron Shore
STEAMBOAT LINE,

Will be composed during the Season of 1868 of the following well-known, first-class, new side wheel Steamers:

CITY OF SANDUSKY, Capt. Henry Fall,
will leave Fridays;

CITY OF TOLEDO, Capt. Selah Dustin,
will leave Wednesdays;

SUSAN WARD, - - - Capt. Wm. Comer,
will leave Tuesdays, Thursdays, and Saturdays,

For Saginaw, Bay City, East Tawas, Tawas City, Port Austin, Huron City, Port Hope, Sand Beach, Rock Falls, Forestville, Forester, Port Sanilac, Lexington, Port Huron, and all other Lake Shore ports.

☞ **All these Boats leave dock foot of Bates St. each day at 2 o'clock P. M.**
FREIGHTS RECEIVED AT ALL TIMES.

For all further information apply to
CHAS. BEWICK, Agent, foot of Bates Street, Detroit.

Reproduction of a handbill circulated in 1868.
—*Capt. F. E. Hamilton Collection.*

PIONEER LINE
FOR LAKE SUPERIOR.
1868.   1868.

THE NEW, STAUNCH & ELEGANT STEAMER

METEOR,

THOMAS WILSON, Master,

WILL LEAVE CLEVELAND,	WILL LEAVE DETROIT,
On the following days, at	On the following days, at
8 O'CLOCK, P. M.	**10 O'CLOCK, P. M.**

Wednesday, May 20.	Wednesday, Aug. 12.	Thursday, May 21.	Thursday, Aug. 13.
Wednesday, June 3.	Wednesday, Aug. 26.	Thursday, June 4.	Thursday. Aug. 27.
Wednesday, June 17.	Wednesday, Sept. 9.	Thursday, June 18.	Thursday, Sept. 10.
Wednesday, July 1.	Wednesday, Sept. 23.	Thursday, July 2.	Thursday, Sept. 24.
Wednesday, July 15.	Wednesday, Oct. 7.	Thursday, July 16.	Thursday, Oct. 8.
Wednesday, July 29.		Thursday, July 30.	

☞ Calling at Port Huron and Sarnia on the next morning after leaving Detroit.

HANNA & CO., Agents, Cleveland, O.
BUCKLEY & CO., Agents, Detroit, Mich.
Or to **J. T. WHITING, Manager, foot First Street, Detroit, Mich.**

1868.   1868.

STEAMER KEWEENAW

Capt. ALBERT STEWART.

For Superior City, and all other Lake Superior Ports.

LEAVES CLEVELAND.		LEAVES DETROIT.	
Wedns'y Eve., May 13	Wedns'y Eve., Aug. 5	Thrsd'y Eve., May 14	Thrsd'y Eve., Aug. 6
" " 27	" " 19	" " 28	" " 20
" " June 10	" " Sept. 2	" " June 11	" " Sept. 3
" " 24	" " 16	" " 25	" " 17
" " July 8	" " 30	" " July 9	" " Oct. 1
" " 22	" " Oct. 14	" " 23	" " 15

The Keweenaw touches at Port Huron and Sarnia on the morning after leaving Detroit,

BRADY & CO., Detroit,   ⎫ AGENTS.
HANNA & CO., Cleveland, ⎭

EBER WARD, Detroit, Owner,

Reproduction of a handbill circulated in 1868.
—*Capt. F. E. Hamilton Collection.*

Claimed to be the oldest ship in the world while afloat, the Australian Convict Ship *Success* lies sunken in the harbor of Sandusky, Ohio, during the summer of 1944, awaiting removal. She was built in 1790 at Burma to be used in the merchant trade, but later was fitted as prison ship to sail between England and Australia. For many years she has been in the waters of the Great Lakes, and may end her days there.

—*Photo gift of Mr. W. G. Schwer.*

MEMORIES OF THE LAKES

ABOVE—Broadside view of ancient prison ship *Success* on display in the 1930's at foot of Superior Avenue, Cleveland, Ohio.

BELOW—Blunt bow of the convict ship *Success* taken while the vessel was on display at East Ninth Street Pier in Cleveland, about 1940. Note the figurehead of a comely maiden adorning the bow and overhanging the water. Such embellishments were supposed to bring the ship good luck.

Detroit, Monroe and Toledo

The Splendid Low Pressure Steamboat.

ARROW,

CAPT. J. W. KEITH,

Leaves Detroit every Monday, Wednesday and Friday,
at 9 o'clock, A. M.   Leaves Toledo every Tuesday,
Thursday and Saturday, connecting at Monroe, each way,
with the M.S.R.R. line Steamers for Buffalo, and
also the Express train of Cars for Chicago

G. TYLER, Clerk.

Early steamer *Arrow*, believed to be the first steamboat of that name on the Great Lakes, was built of wood at Trenton, Michigan, in 1848. She was condemned at Green Bay, Wisconsin, in 1863. The ad inset appeared about 1855. A staunch craft and a dependable skipper brought good business to the boat line. It was the custom in those days to give publicity to both ship and master. This ad pertained to the early sidewheel steamer *Arrow* when this vessel operated on the route mentioned. Picture owned by Detroit Historical Society.

MEMORIES OF THE LAKES

TOP—An early Detroit passenger steamboat, the *Pearl* (first) was built at Newport, Michigan, (now Marine City) in 1851. The photo was taken in 1867. She was dismantled in 1869.—*From collection of Capt. F. E. Hamilton.*

MIDDLE—Steamer *Merchant.* First iron merchant vessel built on the Great Lakes was launched at Buffalo in 1862. She was lost in Lake Michigan in 1875 off Racine, Wisconsin. Her engines were salvaged and placed in the steamer *A. L. Hopkins.*   —*From collection of Louis Baus.*

BOTTOM—Sidewheel passenger steamer *Evening Star* was built in 1866 at East Saginaw, Michigan. At the time this picture was taken she was operating on Lake Erie, between Sandusky, Kelleys Island, and Put-in-Bay.
                —*From collection of W. A. McDonald.*

MEMORIES OF THE LAKES

TOP—One of the early lake schooners, the *Josephine Dresden,* was built in 1852 at Michigan City, Indiana. She was a small craft, only 95 feet long, but served a long and useful career floating hundreds of various cargoes up and down the Great Lakes. She is shown here at a dock in Sheboygan, Wisconsin. *—Louis Baus collection.*

BOTTOM—An early Canadian passenger and freight steamer, the *City of London,* built in 1865 and sailed for several years on Georgian Bay. She burned at Collins Inlet, Ontario, on August 20, 1875.

—Huron Institute collection.

Ornate propeller steamer *Atlantic* served the passenger and package freight trade for many years. Built at Cleveland in 1863, she was 176 feet long and 28 feet beam. This photo was taken in 1894 at St. Ignace, Michigan, when the ship was in the Grummond Line and plying between Cleveland, Toledo, Detroit, Alpena, Mackinac Island and St. Ignace. She had staterooms on both sides of the cabin and a long dining table in the center of the cabin. Everything was served family style.

—*Louis Baus collection.*

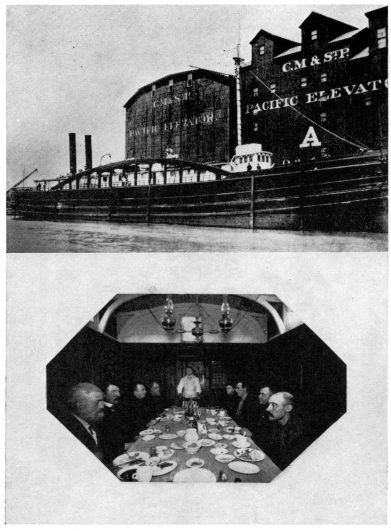

TOP—Steamer *Dean Richmond,* typical arch type wooden steamship of her day, was built at Cleveland in 1864, and was 238 feet long and 35 feet beam. She was lost with all hands the night of October 14, 1893, in Lake Erie off Dunkirk, N. Y., during a raging gale.

BOTTOM—Quaint oil lamps securely fastened to the cabin ceiling illuminated the officers' interesting dining room aboard the steamer *Dean Richmond.* Great Lakes ships have long been famous for their excellent cuisine.
—C. W. Branch collection.

TOP—Windjammers competed with steamers in the early days of Great Lakes shipping. Here is the schooner *Amaranth*, built in 1864 at Milan, Ohio, that had an enviable record for sturdiness and reliability. Early schooners frequently would beat their rival steamers to their destinations. From a drawing by C. W. Norton, and now owned by the Milan, Ohio, Public Library.

BOTTOM—During the days of the Civil War this sidewheel steamer, the *Philo Parsons,* ran between Detroit and Sandusky. In 1864 she figured in an exciting act of piracy. The complete story is related in Chapter Five of this book. From a drawing by C. W. Norton, and now owned by the Sandusky, Ohio, Public Library.

The propeller steamer *St. Albans* was one of a large fleet of similar ships that offered travelers and shippers frequent service between Lake Ontario and Lake Michigan ports. Here the *St. Albans* is docked in the Cuyahoga River in Cleveland. The ship, the overhead viaduct, and all the buildings shown in the photograph are now gone. Only the river remains.

—*From Louis Baus collection.*

Victim of a collision in 1865 off Alpena, Michigan, the passenger and freight steamer *Pewabic* proved to be the object of sunken treasure hunters in later years. The story of the ship is related in Chapter Six of this book.

The schooner *Oak Leaf* was one of the better known sailing vessels of her day. The 188-foot craft was launched on April 14, 1866, by E. M. Peck at Cleveland. Inset of Captain Hugh Morrison, her hardy one-armed skipper. From a drawing by Charles W. Norton, owned by Mr. Robert G. Morrison of Cleveland, grandson of the captain.

MEMORIES OF THE LAKES

TOP—Powerful towing tug *Samson* built in 1866 at Detroit. Typical of many such craft that flourished in the colorful days of the sailing ships of the Great Lakes.

MIDDLE—Canadian passenger and freight steamers *Asia* and *Ontario* taken at Kincardine, Ontario. The story of the *Asia* is related in Chapter Eight of this book. The *Ontario* was built in 1874 at Chatham, Ontario, and was lost in 1899 in Lake Superior near Michipicoten Island.

—From the Huron Institute collection.

BOTTOM—The sidewheel, arch-type, passenger and freight steamer, *Metropolis,* was built of wood in 1868 at Trenton, Michigan. She had a long career and operated the length and breadth of the Great Lakes. She is shown here at a dock in Duluth shortly after her launching. The *Metropolis* burned at Toledo, Ohio, on June 13, 1902.

MEMORIES OF THE LAKES

TOP—Such ships as the *Quebec* (foreground) and the *Ontario* (background) brought Canadian settlers into the Georgian Bay and Sault Ste. Marie territories. Both steamers were built in 1874 and served the Ontario lake ports just prior to the turn of the century.

BOTTOM—The ornate wooden, propeller type steamer, *City of Traverse,* in a lock at the Soo. Note the huge wooden anchor stocks extending from the bow, the extensively decorated pilot house with its fancy windows and its big ornamental eagle, also the giant arches amidships which were to strengthen the vessel, and the two smoke stacks placed athwartships. The *City of Traverse* was built in 1870 at Cleveland, and was 214 feet long and 33 feet beam.

Sailors' Floating Bethel and Free Reading Room at a dock in the Cuyahoga River at Cleveland, about 1870. Chapter Ten of this book relates the story of this interesting little craft. Inset of Chaplain John David Jones, founder of the Bethel.
—*Louis Baus collection.*

TOP—The *India,* one of the famous Lake Triplets, early iron passenger and package freight steamers of the Great Lakes. The *China* and *Japan* were similar ships. Their story is told in Chapter Three of this book.

BOTTOM—The same ship as above, reconditioned, with new owners and under a different name—*City of Ottawa.* This picture was taken about 1908, by Pesha, noted photographer of the Saint Clair River District.

MEMORIES OF THE LAKES

TOP—Interior view of the main cabin aft of the steamer *Japan*. Extreme end was known as the Ladies' Cabin and contained a grand piano, many comfortable chairs, a large mirror, and a thick carpet.

BOTTOM—Engine room of the *Japan*. Part of her deck cargo of filled bags can be seen piled high through the open doorway at right.
—Both photos gift of Captain R. W. England.

TOP—Lake Michigan steamer *Oconto*, the twenty-fourth ship in the old Goodrich Transit Company's fleet. Built in 1872 at Manitowoc, Wisconsin, her engine came from an earlier Goodrich steamer, the *Skylark*. She left Lake Michigan for Detroit owners in 1883 and was lost three years later in the St. Lawrence River.

MIDDLE—Passenger and freight steamer *Mary Ward*. Her story is told in Chapter Eight of this book.

BOTTOM—Steamers *Nahant* and *Westford* in winter quarters at Detroit about 1880. The *Nahant* is recalled as having a very loud steam exhaust, and when navigating in harbors made quite a commotion. Both wooden ships came to a fiery end many miles apart. The *Nahant* burned at Escanaba, Michigan, on November 29, 1897, in below zero temperature, and the *Westford* burned on May 27, 1904, in Georgian Bay. Photo owned by Detroit Historical Society and obtained from W. A. McDonald.

Famous old two-master, *Lyman M. Davis*, veteran of sixty years of lake service. Built in 1873 at Muskegon, Michigan, she was burned as a spectacle off Toronto, Ontario, in 1933.

—*J. B. Bald collection.*

TOP—One of the larger sailing craft, the *J. I. Case,* was built in 1874 at Manitowoc, Wisconsin. For about a half century she operated successfully on the Great Lakes. Her days ended by being intentionally scuttled in deep water in the St. Lawrence River near Quebec.

BOTTOM—Schooner *Two Fannies* at dock, from an old photograph. She was built in 1872 at Peshtigo, Wisconsin, and was 152 feet long and 30 feet beam. She went to pieces in 1879 near Elk Rapids, Michigan, in the East Arm of Grand Traverse Bay.

—*Gift of H. M. Baldwin.*

Schooner *Massasoit*, built in 1874 as the *Jesse Linn*, at Gibralter, Michigan. Her dimensions were 189 feet long and 34 feet beam. See Chapter Twenty-eight in this book for further story. Reproduced from a detailed drawing by Billy Young, one of her crew; presented by him to Captain and Mrs. Charles L. Goodsite, and later presented by them to the author.

MEMORIES OF THE LAKES

TOP—Sidewheel, arch type, passenger and freight steamer, *Chicago*. She was the twenty-seventh ship of the old Goodrich Transit Company fleet that operated on Lake Michigan. Built in 1874 at Manitowoc, Wisconsin, from parts of the steamer *Manitowoc*, she lasted forty-five years, being dismantled in August, 1919.

MIDDLE—Wooden steamer *D. F. Rose*, 140 feet long by 26 feet beam, was built in 1868 at Marine City, Michigan. Boats of this type were known as "rabbits" by their sailors. They were a handy type of freight vessel, particularly in the Detroit and St. Clair Rivers. The *D. F. Rose* operated for over two score years.

BOTTOM— For thirty-six years the steamer *Oscoda* hauled cargoes up and down the Great Lakes. She was one of a great fleet of similar craft known as "lumber hookers" and now completely extinct. Built in 1878 at St. Clair, Michigan, she was 175 feet long and 32 feet beam. She ended her days on treacherous Pelkie Reef, about fifty miles east of Manistique, Michigan, in northern Lake Michigan. Her crew escaped the wreck in one of the most thrilling experiences in the annals of lake history.

—Wm. A. McDonald collection.

An early *Maid of the Mist*, operating on the thrilling trip to the foot of Niagara Falls. Probably the most widely known small steamer in the world. This service has been successfully maintained for many years, and is still a foremost Niagara Falls attraction. Pesha photo.

—*C. W. Branch collection.*

MEMORIES OF THE LAKES

TOP—Shipwreck was the fate of many of the Great Lakes windjammers. Here a big four-master is on the beach following a storm. Note the common distress signal of the sea—the U. S. flag flown upside down—and the forms of the men in the rigging. The photo is believed to be that of the schooner *J. H. Rutter*, in difficulty near Ludington, Michigan.

—J. W. Bald collection.

MIDDLE—Winter travel on the Great Lakes was subject to long delays due to the ship becoming wedged in thick ice. Here the sidewheeler *Flora* is held fast while her passengers stand about her on the ice and watch her progress. At the time this picture was taken the *Flora* was in the Grummond's Mackinac Line trading between Toledo, Detroit, Alpena, and Mackinac.

—C. W. Branch collection.

BOTTOM—A group of steamers clustered about an early ore and coal dock on the upper lakes. The *Gazelle* (in foreground) was built in 1873 at Detroit. The *Nyack* (broadside in background) was built in 1878 at Buffalo. She had a long career on the Great Lakes, lasting around three score years. She was a popular ship in the Crosby Transportation Company fleet on Lake Michigan in the years just following the turn of the century.

The *David Dows* was the largest sailing vessel ever to ply the waters of the Great Lakes. Her dimensions were: 265.4 feet long, 37.6 feet beam, and 18.1 feet deep. Her gross tonnage was 1,418.63, and net tonnage 1,347.7. She was built at Toledo, Ohio, in 1861, for the iron ore and coal trade. Later she was converted into a tow barge and as such foundered in Lake Michigan on Thanksgiving morning, 1889.

—*From a painting by Loudon Wilson.*

TOP—Sixty-seven years ago—in 1879—the trim sidewheel steamboat *Grace McMillen* was launched at Wyandotte, Michigan. Her name was later changed to *Idlewild*. As such she served out of Detroit for many years. When this picture was taken she was operating in the Star Line between Port Huron and Detroit. Her dimensions were 186 feet long, and 26 feet beam.

BOTTOM—Steamer (also called "steambarge" in its day) *Columbia*, an early type of bulk freighter designed for sails to supplement its steam power. She was built in 1881 at Cleveland and was 235 feet in length and 35 feet beam. From a drawing by V. D. Nickerson, owned by the Public Library of Milan, Ohio.

Something of the vastness of the lakes and the sky is expressed in this moonlight view of a big three-masted schooner becalmed on Georgian Bay.
—*J. W. Bald collection.*

MEMORIES OF THE LAKES

TOP—Canadian sidewheel passenger and freight steamer *Waubuno* taken at Collingwood, Ontario. The story of her tragic ending is told in Chapter Eight of this book.　　—*J. W. Bald collection.*

BOTTOM—This huge 3,240-pound anchor was picked up from the bottom of Ashtabula Harbor on July 24, 1939, by the dredge *Mogul*. There is nothing to indicate what ship lost it. Markings on the anchor are believed to show that it was cast in the U. S. Navy Yard at Washington in 1837. The frame of the picture was made from parts of the anchor stock. The anchor now rests at the U. S. Coast Guard Station in Ashtabula.　　—*Photo gift of Captain C. F. Meyers.*

TOP—A very interesting type of early Great Lakes steam freighter was the *W. P. Thew.* She was built of wood in 1884 at Lorain, Ohio, and was 132 feet long and 24 feet beam. She had a gross tonnage of 403.

BOTTOM—Wreck of the Canadian passenger steamer *Algoma* on Isle Royale, in Lake Superior. Built in Scotland, the ship was sailed across the Atlantic and into the Great Lakes. In a violent storm on November 7, 1885, the *Algoma* struck and pounded to pieces with the loss of thirty-eight lives.

—*J. W. Bald collection.*

111

Reproduction of a handbill of Put-In-Bay steamers circulated in 1875. One of the original hand-bills hangs in a frame on the office wall of Mr. Oliver S. Dustin, of the Ashley & Dustin Steamer Line, in Detroit.

MEMORIES OF THE LAKES

TOP—A typical bulk freighter of her day was the steamer *Iron King*. With her consort, the barge *Iron Queen,* they were a familiar sight along the lake lanes at the turn of the century. Both were built in 1887 at Detroit.

—F. T. Patyk collection.

BOTTOM—The wooden steamer *John C. Gault* served the needs of the Wabash Railroad from its launching at Buffalo in 1881, until the railroad sold the ship in 1906. It was later renamed *Felix Cabray* and went to the Atlantic Coast. Brought back to the lakes after a few years, it went again to the Atlantic. The ship foundered on February 27, 1916, off Cape Hatteras.

—Charles F. Mensing photo.

TOP—Iron hulls began to appear more prominently around 1885 when the *Darius Cole* was built in Cleveland. She was 215 feet overall in length and 57 feet beam over the guards. In 1907 she was renamed the *Huron,* and in 1923 the *Colonial.* She burned in Lake Erie on September 1, 1926, off Barcelona, New York, with the loss of three lives. She is shown here as she traded between Toledo, Detroit and Port Huron.

—W. A. McDonald collection.

BOTTOM—The Canadian passenger and freight steamer *Alberta* leaving her dock in Chicago about 1930. A sister ship *Athabasca* was similiar in appearance. Both were built in Scotland in 1883 and sailed across the Atlantic into the Great Lakes, where they have operated for over 60 years. They were sold in 1945 for salt water service.

A busy dock scene at Erie, Pennsylvania, about 1889. Clustered about the dock (in right foreground) are the schooners *Henry C. Richards*, *Homer D. Alverson*, and *Saveland* (next to steamer). The steamer (center background) is unidentified. The schooner *Hattie Wells* is the first boat at the left (foreground). The "dock boss" stands at lower right.

—*Gift of Captain Wm. P. Benham.*

115

TOP—The Canadian passenger and freight propeller steamer *Pacific,* a crack liner of her day (1883 to 1898) is shown in a lock at Sault Ste. Marie, Michigan, along with a sailing vessel carrying a cargo of lumber. The *Pacific* burned at her dock in Collingwood, Ontario, on November 3rd, 1898.

BOTTOM—Another of the extinct lake "lumber hookers," the *Philetus Sawyer*. Wood lath, a product almost forgotten by the building trades in 1946, makes up her cargo. Piled higher than her cabins, the *Philetus Sawyer* floated the products of the forests to the markets. Built in 1884 at Green Bay, Wisconsin, the ship was active in the lumber trade on the Great Lakes for many years.

MEMORIES OF THE LAKES

TOP—Many combination passenger and freight steamers plied the Great Lakes in the eighties. The *Fannie C. Hart* of The Green Bay Transportation Company fleet ran between Green Bay ports and Mackinac and Sault Ste. Marie. She was built in 1888 at Manitowoc, Wisconsin, and was 142 feet long and 30 feet beam.

BOTTOM—Many scenic lake and river trips now forgotten, were the regular commercial routes of the past. Here is the Canadian steamer *City of Chatham* wending her way down the fruit-lined banks of the Thames River, into Lake St. Clair, and thence to Detroit. She was built in 1888 and is today but a memory. Because of the reflections in the quiet water, the picture is almost the same if turned upside down.

The schooner *Cora A.* was the last commercial windjammer to be built on the Great Lakes. She was built in 1889 at Manitowoc, Wisconsin, and was 146 feet long and 31 feet beam. In 1916 she went to salt water and was lost in 1923 on the Atlantic Coast. The picture shows her about 1914 as she was light, leaving Fort William, Ontario, via the Mission Entrance. The Welcome Islands are in the background.

MEMORIES OF THE LAKES

TOP—The *Minnedosa*, built in Canada in 1890 and claimed to be the only four-masted Canadian schooner to sail the Great Lakes. She was 245 feet long and 45 feet beam. She foundered in Lake Huron in October, 1905.   —*J. W. Bald collection.*

MIDDLE—Schooner towing proved to be big business in the harbors and rivers during the sailing vessel days. Here is shown the tug *Goldsmith* with six windjammers in her tow. They are (in order):*Fearless, York State, Eva Fuller, J. N. Porter, Butcher Boy* and *George W. Douseman.*

BOTTOM—Seaworthiness is vital to Great Lakes freighters. Here is the steamer *Maruba* rolling and tossing in a heavy sea on Lake Huron in November, 1904. The *Maruba* was built in 1890 at Cleveland, and was 290 feet long and 40 feet beam. When Cleveland filled in its lakefront about 1938, the *Maruba* lay abandoned and in the way of making the fill. Earth was dumped completely around the ship and she was thus dismantled, surrounded entirely by dry land.   ---*Capt. W. J. Taylor photograph.*

Passenger steamer *Frank E. Kirby* on Lake Erie. Inset shows her propulsion machinery removed after the vessel had burned. The story of the ship is told in Chapter Twenty-one of this book.

—*Photo gift of Mr. R. G. Morrison.*
—*Inset gift of Mr. G. E. Bennett.*

MEMORIES OF THE LAKES

TOP—The launching of a ship is always a momentous occasion. Here the
wooden hull of the freighter *Wm. B. Morley* is sliding sideways down the
ways into the waters of the Belle River at Marine City, Michigan. The
year is 1888. Later her name was changed to *Caledonia,* and still later to
Gales Staples. The ship stranded at Grand Marais, Michigan, on October
1st, 1918.   —*W. A. McDonald collection.*

MIDDLE—Large and small steamers at Lakeside, Ohio. The picture, taken
about 1900, shows the small steamer *Osceola* in the foreground, and astern
of her is the big steamer *Metropolis,* while heading lakeward is the steamer
A. Wehrle, Jr.   —*Louis Baus collection.*

BOTTOM—A Great Lakes three-masted schooner bound down on Lake
Superior about fifty years ago. Her identity is not known.
                                                   —*Gift of Captain R. W. England.*

121

MEMORIES OF THE LAKES

TOP—The bulk freighter *Alexander McDougall,* a modified type of whale-back steamer. At the close of World War II, along with twenty-five other freighters, she was consigned to the scrap pile. Her story is told in Chapter Nineteen of this book.　　　*—Edwin Wilson photograph.*

BOTTOM—The barge *Alexander Holley.* She exemplifies the Great Lakes-originated whaleback type of ship, now almost a complete memory. At first the whalebacks were built as barges, and later as steamers. The story of this interesting type of ship is found in Chapter Nineteen of this book.
　　　　　　　　　　　—Edwin Wilson photograph.

MEMORIES OF THE LAKES

Making a forest of their tall masts, these sailing ships are shown thickly clustered in their winter quarters at a lower lake port. Here repairs were made and gear overhauled. This picture was taken about 1900.

—*Louis Baus collection.*

MEMORIES OF THE LAKES

TOP—The steamer *Lakeland* was converted into a passenger boat from the freighter *Cambria*. On December 4, 1924, while enroute from Chicago to Detroit, she sank in Lake Michigan, about nine miles off Sturgeon Bay Ship Canal, in 185 feet of water. No lives were lost. As the *Cambria* she was built in 1887 at Cleveland.

—*C. W. Branch collection.*

BOTTOM—Passenger steamer *George M. Cox* high on Rock of Ages, off the western end of Isle Royale, Lake Superior. She ran on the treacherous reef on May 27, 1933. All passengers and crew were rescued. Shortly after this picture was taken the ship slid off the rock and sank in the deep water that surrounds the Rock. She was never recovered. The steamer was built in 1901 at Toledo, Ohio, as the *Puritan*.

—*W. A. McDonald collection.*

Harbor Beach, Michigan, last harbor of refuge on the western shore of Lake Huron for upbound ships before they crossed the wide expanse of open waters where Saginaw Bay joins Lake Huron. Large fleets often tied up there awaiting weather. Steamers, tugs, barges, and schooners, are shown in shelter from a bad lake blow about 1892. It is recalled that around 110 various craft were in port at the time this picture was taken. Such fleets would sometimes stay a week in port awaiting weather. Local merchants did a thriving business on such occasions.

—*Photo gift of Mr. A. F. Tschirhart.*

Whaleback steamer *Samuel Mather* bringing a cargo of iron ore to a dock up the Cuyahoga River at Cleveland, about 1900. The tug *Frank W.* is assisting. Wooden steamer *Wm. J. Averell* at dock at extreme left. The *Samuel Mather* later became the *Clifton* and was lost with all hands in Lake Huron on September 22, 1924. See Chapter Nineteen on "Whalebacks" in this book.

—*Louis Baus collection.*

MEMORIES OF THE LAKES

TOP—A boat familiar to Chicagoans traveling to St. Joseph, Michigan, and other Lake Michigan ports in the years around 1920. The steamer *City of Holland* of the Graham & Morton Line was formerly the *City of Mackinac* of the D & C Lines. Adverse business conditions caused the ship to be laid up and eventually dismantled. She was built in 1893 at Wyandotte, Michigan.

BOTTOM—The tanker barge *Cleveco* is one of the more recent memories of the Great Lakes. Enroute to Cleveland from Toledo with a full cargo of fuel oil, on December 2, 1942, her tug, *Admiral,* foundered before dawn a few miles off Cleveland. The *Cleveco,* with no power of her own, was forced along by a violent storm. It is believed she sank late that afternoon. All hands on the *Admiral* and *Cleveco* were lost—32 in all. The vessels still lie on the bottom of Lake Erie.   —*Captain W. J. Taylor photo.*

Detroit's popular excursion steamer *Tashmoo* operated out of that city from 1900 until 1936. Thousands upon thousands of the Automobile City's folks found pleasure and relaxation upon her broad decks.

The finish of the famous one hundred mile race between the steamers *Tashmoo* and *City of Erie* run on June 4, 1901, from Cleveland, Ohio, to Erie, Pennsylvania. It was the greatest sporting event ever held on the Great Lakes. The *City of Erie* won by only forty-five seconds. Steamers in the picture, left to right, *Tashmoo*, *Pleasure*, *City of Buffalo*, and the winner, *City of Erie* (in smoke).

—*Louis Baus collection.*

One of the most popular passenger steamers of her day, the *Octorara* ran from Buffalo to Duluth, making calls at the larger ports enroute. The sister ships *Octorara*, *Tionesta* and *Juniata* provided regular and dependable passenger and freight service the length of the lakes. They ceased operation in 1937. The *Octorara* lay idle at Buffalo until the beginning of World War II, when the government took her over. She was sent to salt water and became a U. S. Army transport, operating in the Pacific. She is at present in this service.

TOP—Giant waves crashed over the ill-fated freighter *Mataafa* during the 1905 blow at Duluth, driving the ship into shallow water near the shore, where she settled on the bottom. Read Chapter Twenty-four of this book.
—*McKenzie photograph.*
BOTTOM—Beaten and broken the *Mataafa* lies within sight of the city of Duluth. Nine men lost their lives in the wreck. The ship was subsequently raised and returned to service.
—*McKenzie photograph.*

Where early lake steamers and canal boats met. Each helped the other to prosper. The picture shows Cleveland Harbor about 1870.
—*Louis Baus collection.*

TOP—Steel freighter *William B. Davock* lost in the 1940 Armistice Day storm on Lake Michigan. For the story of this storm read Chapter Twenty-nine of this book.   —*Young photograph.*

BOTTOM—Canadian freighter *Anna C. Minch* also lost in the 1940 Armistice Day storm on Lake Michigan.   —*Young photograph.*

Man-made Kafralu Island in beautiful Sandusky Bay off Lake Erie. The tale of this island is told in Chapter Twenty-three of this book.

—*Photo gift of Mrs. L. E. Wagner.*

The steamer *Jack* recalls several memories to the men of the lakes. Her building in 1919 at Lorain, Ohio, brings forth thoughts of World War I, and the consequent rush of activities on the Great Lakes. The *Jack*, built as the *Lake Freso*, was known as a "Welland Canaler." Refer to Chapter Twenty-seven. She also recalls the "Poker Fleet" of the lakes, with the ships: *Ace*, *King*, *Queen*, *Ten*, and *Nine*, handling package freight. The *Jack* went to salt water in the service of the government at the start of World War II, as did all the "Welland Canalers" on the Great Lakes.
—*Captain W. J. Taylor photograph.*

The steamer *Greater Buffalo*, luxurious Great Lakes liner, is today but a memory. The *Greater Buffalo* and her twin sister, the *Greater Detroit*, were the largest sidewheel steamers in the world. Both were built in 1924 at Lorain, Ohio. They operated chiefly on an overnight run between Detroit and Buffalo. In 1942 the *Greater Buffalo* was converted into a "flat-top" by the U. S. Navy and used for flyer training. She was then renamed the *Sable*. The *Greater Detroit* remained on the Detroit and Buffalo run.

—*Kenneth Smith photo*

The steamer *Seeandbee*, launched November 9, 1912, at Wyandotte, Michigan, was for many years the largest sidewheel steamer in the world. Operating chiefly between Cleveland and Buffalo, she carried large crowds. Later she sailed on week cruises between Chicago and Buffalo. In 1942 she was converted into a "flat-top" by the U. S. Navy and used to train pilots in carrier landings. Her name was then changed to *Wolverine*.
—*Captain W. J. Taylor photograph.*

Put-In-Bay Harbor, South Bass Island, Lake Erie, as seen from atop the Perry Memorial. Many lake memories rest here. Oliver Hazard Perry used this harbor during the War of 1812. Hundreds of ships, now all but forgotten, have brought thousands of vacationists Great Lakes yachtsmen gather here yearly for their regattas. All the steamers shown in this picture, taken about 1937, are memories. The steamer *Goodtime* (in center) was dismantled in 1940, as was the *Chippewa* (left center), and the *Erie Isle*, (docked near the *Goodtime's* bow).

—*Photo gift of Wm. D. Preston.*

A million lake sailor memories rest here. These freighters, anchored in Erie Bay in 1945, were awaiting dismantling. Replaced by larger and faster ships, they were outmoded. Twenty-six steamers in all were so condemned. They were: *Clarence A. Black, Cetus* (formerly *F. W. Gilchrist*), *Corvus* (formerly *J. L. Weeks*), *Cygnus* (formerly *J. C. Gilchrist*), *Robert Fulton, Kickapoo* (formerly *Captain Thomas Wilson*), *George B. Leonard, Mariposa, Maritana, Pentecost Mitchell, Alexander McDougall, William Nottingham, A. W. Osborne* (formerly *Andrew Carnegie*), *Pegasus* (formerly *Wm. H. Gratwick*), *Queen City, Rensselear, Saturn* (formerly *W. Scranton*), *B. Lyman Smith, Monroe C. Smith, Wilbert L. Smith, H. C. Strom* (formerly *A. H. Ferbert* and *A. F. Harvey*), *Superior* (formerly *Richard J. Reiss* and *G. W. Peavey*), *Taurus* (formerly *Perry G. Walker*), *Alex B. Uhrig* (formerly *Centurion*), *Vega* (formerly *Pendennis White*), and *Zenith City*.

—*Louis Baus collection.*

Reproduction of an advertisement and timetable circulated in 1843 regarding Lake Ontario passenger steamers.

—*J. W. Bald collection.*

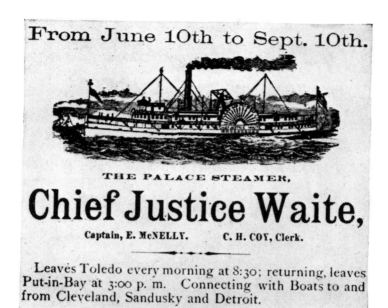

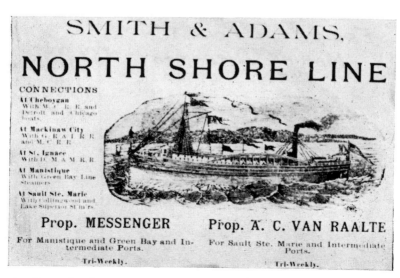

Reproduction of advertisements appearing in periodicals, (top) in 1886, (bottom) in 1884.

Reproduction of a full page advertisement in an 1884 Marine Directory.
—*Courtesy of Wm. D. Preston.*

GOODRICH TRANSPORTATION CO.

A. E. GOODRICH, President, CHICAGO.

T. G. BUTLIN, Supt., CHICAGO.
W. H. WRIGHT, Treas., CHICAGO.
J. SINGLETON, Pass. Agt., CHICAGO.

G. HURSON, Sec. and Agt., MILWAUKEE.
G. W. SCANLAN, Agt., RACINE.
J. W. TOOMBS, Agt., MANITOWOC.

Side-wheel Passenger Steamers

TWICE DAILY

FROM

CHICAGO to RACINE & MILWAUKEE,

Every Morning at 9 o'clock, and every Evening at 8 o'clock, Sunday excepted.

*The Morning Boat goes through to Sheboygan and Manitowoc; also,
on Saturdays at 8 p.m.*

For Ludington and **Manistee** every Morning at 9 o'clock, except Sunday.

For Kewaunee, Sturgeon Bay and Menominee, every Morning at 9 o'clock except Saturdays and Sundays; on Saturdays at 8 p.m.

For Grand Haven, Muskegon, Grand Rapids, Monday, Wednesday and Friday Evenings, at 7 o'clock.

For Frankfort, Pierport, Arcadia, etc., Tuesday and Saturday Mornings at 9 o'clock.

GREEN BAY and ESCANABA ROUTES.

Every Saturday Morning at 9 o'clock,

For West Shore Ports, Washington Island, Fayette, Escanaba (and via Escanaba for Lake Superior Towns), Fish Creek, Ephraim, Ellison's Bay, Green Bay, De Pere, etc.

Office and Docks: Foot of Michigan Avenue, CHICAGO.

Reproduction of a full page advertisement in an 1884 Marine Directory.
—*Courtesy of Wm. D. Preston.*

DISTANCES BETWEEN POINTS ON GREAT LAKES

—*Courtesy U. S. Lake Survey Office.*

mile; if the respective ports measure 116.0 and 115.2, they appear in the table as 116 and 115, a difference of 1 mile; whereas from the next port listed, the distances to the same two points may measure 105.4 and 104.6, and both will appear in the table as 105.

Measurements are by the shortest marked or safe direct courses, starting (unless otherwise noted) from the main entrances between pierheads of breakwaters or piers, or from the principal landings of open roadsteads. Where landings are appreciably remote from protected entrances, the appropriate further distances, if desired, may be ascertained from the harbor descriptions or from charts.

Points in this table are arranged in the order of their location on the several lakes in the following sequence: Lake Superior, Lake Michigan, Lake Huron, Lake Erie, and Lake Ontario.

The distance between any two points appears in the line extending horizontally from the point first in order in the list and in the column headed by the other point.

EXPLANATION

Distances in these tables are expressed to the nearest even statute mile; fractions of 1 mile or more being taken as a full mile and those under the half dropped. The results are, therefore, at times inconsistent by 1 mile in their comparative differences. Thus, measured distances to two given points may differ uniformly by 0.8

	Montreal	Ogdensburg	Kingston	Toronto	Oswego	Rochester	Port Colborne	Buffalo	Erie	Conneaut	Ashtabula	Fairport	Cleveland	Lorain	Toledo	Detroit	Port Huron	Midland	Collingwood	Goderich	Bay City	Alpena	Ludington	Muskegon	Gary	Chicago	Milwaukee	Green Bay	Escanaba	Sault Ste. Marie	Marquette	Houghton	Ashland	Duluth	Two Harbors
Port Arthur	1212	1094	1034	903	1016	965	848	864	795	768	754	729	711	694	658	604	542	539	531	506	505	410	536	587	699	686	621	560	492	273	171	116	164	195	172
Two Harbors	1310	1192	1132	1001	1114	1063	946	963	893	866	852	828	809	792	756	702	640	638	630	604	603	508	634	685	797	785	720	659	590	391	239	157	71	28	
Duluth	1384	1216	1156	1025	1138	1087	970	986	917	890	876	851	833	816	781	726	664	661	653	628	627	532	657	709	820	808	743	682	614	394	261	179	93		
Ashland	1258	1170	1110	979	1092	1041	844	830	806				788	771	734	688	618	616	608	583	581	486	612	663	775	763	698	637	568	385	131	213			
Houghton	1160	1042	982	851	964	913	716	702	678				659	643	606	552	490	488	480	455	453	358	494	535	647	635	570	509	440	221	84				
Marquette	1099	981	921	790	903	852	655	641	616				598	581	545	490	429	426	418	383	391	297	422	474	585	573	508	447	378	159					
Sault Ste. Marie	939	821	761	630	743	692	575	592	522				438	422	385	331	224	265	259	234	232	137	263	314	426	414	349	288	219						
Escanaba	1046	928	868	737	850	799	682	699	629				545	528	492				376	340	339	244	130	181	288	274	201	101							
Green Bay	1115	997	937	806	919	868	751	767	698				615	597	561				444	409	407	313	123	171	272	255	180								
Milwaukee	1176	1058	998	867	980	929	812	828	759				675	658	622				505	470	468	374	97	80	103	85									
Chicago	1241	1123	1063	932	1045	994	877	893	824				740	723	688				570	535	534	439	156	114	25										
Gary	1253	1135	1075	945	1057	1006	889	905	836				752	735	699				582	547	546	451	167	121											
Muskegon	1141	1023	963	832	945	894	777	794	724				640	623	587				471	434	434	339	56												
Ludington	1090	972	912	781	894	843	726	742	673				589	572	536				419	384	383	288													
Alpena	827	709	649	518	631	580	463	479	410				326	309	273				185	124	116														
Bay City	832	714	654	523	636	585	468	494	415				331	314	278				257	137															
Goderich	735	617	557	426	539	488	371	387	318				234	217	181				207																
Collingwood	928	810	750	619	732	681	564	580	511				484	470	446																				
Midland	936	818	758	627	740	689	572	588	519				435	418	382																				
Port Huron	670	552	492	361	474	423	306	322	253				170	152	116																				
Detroit	608	490	430	289	412	361	244	261	191				108	91	54																				
Toledo	601	483	423	292	405	354	237	254	185				96	72																					
Lorain	544	426	366	235	348	297	180	197	124				28																						
Cleveland	524	406	346	215	328	277	160	176	102																										
Fairport	494	376	316	185	298	247	130	146	73																										
Ashtabula	468	350	290	159	272	221	104	119	45																										
Conneaut	456	338	278	147	260	209	92	107	33																										
Erie	429	311	251	120	233	182	65	78																											
Buffalo	386	268	208	77	190	139	22																												
Port Colborne	364	246	186	55	168	117																													
Rochester	266	147	89	95	145																														
Oswego	227	108	55	59																															
Toronto	338		161																																
Kingston	182	63																																	
Ogdensburg	120																																		
Montreal	0																																		

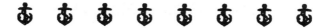

CHAPTER ELEVEN

THE FLOATING BETHEL

Every port where large ships docked in the latter part of the past century had its tough community. The Great Lakes ports were no exception to this situation. A well dressed stranger was usually singled out as having too much cash on his person. It behooved him to look well to his safety for there were plenty of loafers anxious to transfer his wallet to their pockets, and the manner of transfer was usually foul.

The crooked Cuyahoga River oozed its oily way into Lake Erie past the busy waterfront of Cleveland, and many were the holdups and brawls within sight of this river. Whiskey Island, where the river divided as it entered the lake, was as tough a spot in those days as any place on salt water in the world. None but the brave and the fools ventured into Cleveland's "flats" after dark.

As night fell on this section of squalor and dock warehouses, and its saloons and bawdry places lit their gas and oil lamps, so also did competitive lights glow on a little humble vessel moored here or there in the murky Cuyahoga. As far as records go this odd craft had no name. Sailors knew it merely as the *Floating Bethel*. Maybe sixty or so feet long with a substantial beam, a blunt nose and square stern, the *Floating Bethel* was a familiar sight in the Cleveland harbor for many years. She had no means of propulsion. A friendly tug or bum-boat would drag the *Floating Bethel* to the various docks about the harbor, and oftimes her stay would run into months before another shift would be made.

Her interior was one large room having a pulpit near the bow. Chairs and benches accommodated the congregation and served meanwhile the callers who found the daily papers and current magazines brought for their use.

The skipper and owner of this odd craft was one-armed Chaplain John David Jones, a rather short and stocky man with a dignified and priestly mien. He devoted all of his later years to the betterment of the sailormen. Every man about the Cleveland docks knew, liked and respected the chaplain. When only seven years old he went sailing before the mast on lake schooners. He followed the water his entire life. During the Civil War he joined the Navy and went to salt water, but returned to the lakes afterward. The hard life of a windjammer made its mark upon the growing boy and he early learned the evil of the world.

With a great love for drink he became one of the wildest of sailormen. Then came a railroad accident in which he fell under the wheels of a freight train and in which he lost an arm. His life being spared in the accident caused the man to become converted and he vowed to mend his ways and to go forth and help his fellow sailors. In 1868 he began his efforts with the *Floating Bethel*. From the start he had the utmost respect of the waterfront population. Here was a man that had been around. He could handle himself in any situation. If religion helped him it could help others, they reasoned, and many were the converts in Chaplain Jones' meetings.

The good chaplain soon counted among his best friends men of means in the early lake shipping trade, all anxious to improve the lot of the sailor. He became acquainted with police officers, judges, politicians, doctors, clergymen; they were all his friends. He came in contact with many of them in his business of helping the sailor.

He was a strong man physically as well as spiritually, despite the fact that he had but one arm. He could stand his ground in any fracass along the waterfront, and reports persist that he had a standing offer to vanquish any one-armed man that cared to come forth. His eloquence and persuasive manner made him many friends, and his acquired refinement and culture were a surprise to those who met him for the first time. He could preach a sermon that would do credit to any clergyman of the day. His efforts founded a home for friendless children in Cleveland that is still in existence.

City police when called to a waterfront brawl in their high wheeled, horse-drawn patrol wagons would more times than not, turn their "pinches" over to Chaplain Jones. They would reason, and correctly too, that it would save jail costs, court costs, and would do the culprit a lot more good to talk with the chaplain than with the judge.

The *Floating Bethel* became a haven for waterfront transgressors and many a lasting convert did the good chaplain have to his credit.

147

MEMORIES OF THE LAKES

No one recalls just what became of the *Floating Bethel*. Some say that the good skipper had it hauled ashore and mounted on wheels where it served as a revival tabernacle in the more remote spots of the Lake Erie country.

⚓ ⚓ ⚓ ⚓ ⚓ ⚓ ⚓ ⚓

CHAPTER TWELVE

THE OLD SUCCESS

During the years 1943 and 1944 there has lain at a dock in Sandusky Bay that famous old Convict Ship *Success*, acclaimed as the oldest ship afloat. During this time the tired old vessel has taken on more water than her pumps could expel and she has settled slowly on the bottom. Wearily, she rolled over a bit on her port side, snapping her dock lines, and settling down for a well earned rest. Will this be her last rest? Will she be scrapped? Will she be refloated to again cruise about to extol the ghastliness of British convict handling in the early days? Or will she find a niche in the commercial trade? The answer rests with her owners, no doubt depending upon her chances for future industrial success.

The old veteran lies in about eighteen feet of water but much of her is still above the water line. A few steps along a hazardous gangplank and a complete ignoring of a warning sign to "Keep Off" will bring a person to the ancient deck, now slanting precariously. The fresh water of Lake Erie can be heard sloshing about in her hold. Here, standing alone on the rotting deck, the fullness of the ship's life envelopes one.

She was built in the year 1790, seven years before the launching of the famous *U. S. S. Constitution (Old Iron-*

sides), and just nine years after the surrender of Corn-
wallis at Yorktown, ending the Revolutionary War. This
same year saw the creation of the United States Revenue
Marine, our present Coast Guard. World trade was then
in its swaddling clothes. In far off Burma, near the spot
made famous by Kipling's lines, "By the old Moulmain
pagoda, looking eastward to the sea," the keel of the *Success* was laid on the left bank of the Salwin River.

The young city of Moulmain had started on a career of
shipbuilding and the nearby forests of teak and ironwood
furnished the time-resisting wood for its ships. There it
was that the solid teak timber of tremendous proportions
was laid and sister keelsons of almost as great weight began
to form the ship. She was a stout vessel. Her sides were
two feet six inches thick at the bilge. She was made 135
feet in length and 30 feet beam, of around 600 tons. Built
entirely of Burmese teak she was copper fastened and
"trenailed" throughout. Her bows were bluff and her stern
was square cut with quarter galleries, all of which were
painstakingly embellished with elaborate wood carvings,
escutcheons and scrolls. Her figurehead was that of a
beautiful woman, said to represent a British queen.

Into the new ship went everything that an armed East
India merchant ship could boast of. She was outfitted with
bristling brass cannons to protect herself from the dangers
of pirates that lurked along the sea lanes. Her decks were
shaded by expensive cloths under which the rich merchants
of India bargained for their wares; ivory, silks, precious
stones, lead, copper, cotton and rice.

THE OLD SUCCESS

From the time of her launching and until 1802 the *Success* was all that her name implied. She traded back and forth between England and India and other ports. Except for an occasional brush with pirates, which she fortunately always repulsed, the solid little vessel had a peaceful and profitable existence.

It was in 1802 that the British Government chartered the *Success* to transport certain prisoners to penal colonies in Australia. Those were the dark days of civilization and the *Success* carried on in this unhappy trade for forty-nine long years . Indescribable suffering is reported to have existed among the prisoners aboard the ship and many deaths resulted from the treatment and confinement.

In 1851 the *Success* was converted into a floating prison and was permanently stationed in Hobson's Bay, Australia. Here more heinous tortures were inflicted upon the luckless incarcerated individuals. For seventeen years the old ship served as a floating prison. By then the penal system of Australia was revised and the *Success* and her sister prison hulks were ordered abandoned. However, the vessel continued in a lesser degree as a women's punitive reformatory for several years and later a storage ship for ammunition. Eventually orders came for the breaking up of all the floating prison ships, that they might forever pass from the sight of the Australian people.

Somehow, believed due to a clerical error, the *Success* missed the wreckers' tools and stood abandoned in the harbor of Sydney at Fort Jackson. In 1885 the old craft was scuttled and rested on the bottom for five years.

MEMORIES OF THE LAKES

She was not forgotten. In 1890, after her one hundredth birthday, the old ship, still sound, was raised and again floated on the harbor waters. Now she was a show boat. Authentic relics of her barbarian penal days were brought to the *Success* and placed on display. People paid good money to go aboard the old vessel and examine the instruments of torture of her bygone years. She cruised about the Australasian Colonies for a time and then once more set her course for Great Britain. Millions of people visited the old ship in her cruises twice around Great Britain and Ireland. English royalty and members of other European royal families are mentioned as coming aboard the quaint old craft.

The *Success* remained as a show boat in British waters until 1912 when a Yankee skipper, Captain D. H. Smith, bought her. He decided to sail the one hundred and twenty-two year old ship under her own canvas to the United States and there place her on exhibition. This was a very hazardous and daring undertaking, but Captain Smith gathered together a dauntless crew and felt confident that the old *Success* would weather the North Atlantic gales.

On the very same day, April 10, 1912, that the ill-fated liner *Titanic* sailed from Southampton, England, the humble *Success* spread her canvass to the sea winds, leaving Glasson Dock near the port of Liverpool. Four days later the *Titanic* was wrecked by collision with an iceberg on this, her maiden trip, and 1,513 persons perished as the crack new liner sank beneath the waves. Better fortune favored the old *Success*. After a long voyage lasting ninety-six days, she arrived in Boston Harbor. It was truly a memorable trip and much credit is due the captain and crew for the splendid manner in which they handled the old India merchantman across the wild Atlantic and brought her safely into port.

Upon her arrival she was placed on exhibition in Boston and subsequently New York, Philadephia, and many other eastern seaports. Later she made the long trip through the Panama Canal to San Francisco where she was placed in the Panama-Pacific Exposition. There great crowds went aboard the old vessel as she lay at the Fair dock. Later she visited other Pacific-American ports; thence returning through the Canal and into the Gulf of Mexico where she called at New Orleans and the river cities of the Mississippi, Missouri, Illinois and Ohio Rivers.

Again returning to the Gulf she made her way up the Atlantic Coast to the mouth of the St. Lawrence River. She eventually sailed into the Great Lakes in 1924 and there called at the principal ports. Millions more went aboard this interesting old veteran. It is claimed that in her travels over twenty-one million people have trod her decks. There is no denying the fact that the *Success* did get around.

In June 1939 the old ship was brought for the third time to Cleveland and placed on exhibition at the East Ninth Street Pier. She was at that time owned by Cleveland interests. After a lengthy stay in that city she was taken to Sandusky and there tied up. While there her ill luck befell her and once again the old craft sank. The sight of the old hulk lying awry makes one stop and ponder.

There lies the ship that men fashioned from solid teak in far off Burma 154 years ago; that has been attacked by pirates; that has transported thousands of prisoners to infamous penal colonies; that has housed many of Australia's worst criminals; that has sailed alone across the Atlantic when over one hundred years old; that has cruised into almost every port in the United States, England, Scotland, Ireland, and Australia; that has had millions of visitors aboard, including nobility.

Yes, truly, the old *Success* has been around a bit!

Note: The *Success* was later floated and towed near Port Clinton, Ohio, where, on July 4, 1946, she caught fire and burned to the water's edge.

CHAPTER THIRTEEN

OUR SON

Fifty-five years is a long time for a wooden vessel to withstand the tempests of the Great Lakes, especially for a windjammer, where the stress and strain of sudden gales force every foot of the ship to its utmost. The schooner *Our Son* lasted that long and ended her days "in the harness" with a load of pulpwood aboard, trying to make a Lake Michigan port.

To the *Our Son* goes the credit of being the last of the Great Lakes-built windjammer fleet of thousands of such vessels that for several decades carried the growing commerce of these lakes. With their white sails spread to the breeze, they presented a picture never to be seen in modern times. From Duluth to the St. Lawrence they plied their various trades—package freight, bulk cargo, passengers. In fact, everything imaginable was water-bourne in these sailing craft.

With the opening of the New York State Canal in 1826 and the Ohio Canal in 1830, the freight and produce of the inland country was brought by canal boats to the lower lake ports and transferred to these schooners; thence to many distant markets along the lakes. The first locomotive ever to huff and puff in the great railroad city of Chicago was brought there aboard a lake schooner during the year

155

1837. Another similar engine was unloaded later in Manitowoc from the deck of a schooner. Dynamite was not an unusual item of cargo upbound for the fearless boats, to be used in the fast growing mining operations at the head of the lakes. Lumber was brought downbound to the growing cities of the lower lakes, while coal was floated in full cargoes upbound. The Great Lakes windjammer played a big part in the general development of the Middle West, and the *Our Son* outlived them all.

She was built in 1875 by Captain Henry Kelley at Lorain, Ohio, then known as Black River. Captain Kelley owned a considerable fleet of schooners on the lakes. Prominent among them was the *Oak Leaf*, a smart craft ably commanded by the hardy, one-armed skipper of those days, Captain Hugh Morrison, of Milan, Ohio. The Kelley fleet were always trim and well kept vessels and their crews were famous for their expert seamanship.

As the *Our Son*, at that time unnamed, lay almost completed on the shipbuilder's ways on the bank of the Black River, a young son of Captain Kelley fell into the water while playing about the new boat and was drowned. In his memory the new schooner was named *Our Son*. Another oddity about this name is that it stayed with the ship to her end. Most vessels during their careers have a change of name, some as many as a half dozen, but in the long life of the *Our Son* she always carried the same name. That, in a way, probably accounted for much of the popularity of the ship.

The *Our Son* measured 182 feet over all, 35 feet beam and 13 feet deep. She cost about $6,000 to build, and she could haul about 1,000 tons of iron ore or 40,000 bushels of grain to a cargo. With a favorable breeze she could travel 12 to 15 miles per hour. When new, and for some time later, she was barque-rigged, carrying a foremast, mainmast and mizzenmast, but was square-rigged on the foremast only. She was rated as one of the finest schooners on the Great Lakes. On her lower topsail were painted the large black letters O. S., by which she was readily recognized many miles away.

When the new schooner started hauling ore and grain on the lakes, the era of the wooden ship was at its peak. The windjammer was king. Steam was used only when the wind was unfavorable, and then it was in the form of a barking tug, engaged to tow the schooner out of a harbor or a river and into the open lake.

But steam was a competitor to be seriously reckoned with. It developed and proved highly dependable. It also made faster average time. The early sailors on the *Our Son* would line the rail to watch a "smoker", as they termed the early steamers, go past. In her latter days, the crews of the steamers lined the rail when meeting the windjammer. Many schooners were cut down into barges and were towed behind a steamer. The *Our Son* did her turn at this. Her rig was altered, but not completely done away with, and she could carry sails upon fairly short notice.

She made a memorable run down the length of Lake Erie from the mouth of the Detroit River to Buffalo on one of the wildest nights of the Big Storm in November 1913. She was then in the command of Captain Charles L. Goodsite and in tow of the steamer *C. H. Green* with the schooner *Genoa* also in the same tow. Captain Goodsite afterwards told of the heavy wooden planks that made up her deck cargo being lifted bodily by the wind and swirled away in the howling gale to be quickly lost to sight in the blinding snow. That night proved that the builders had put real quality of material and workmanship into the *Our Son* when she was built back there in Black River.

But the transition from wind to steam was inevitable. The *Our Son* saw the steamer improve and grow ever larger. She also saw her windjammer contemporaries pass out, one by one, until at last she was carrying on alone, the only remaining cargo sailing vessel traveling the Great Lakes. By this time she was hauling cordwood into Muskegon, Michigan, from the Canadian shore around Manitoulin Island and northern Lake Huron.

On September 26, 1930, Lake Michigan was in a gale of wind. The waves ran high. Mid-afternoon found Captain Fred Nelson, a veteran of fifty-nine years of sailing on salt and fresh water, coaxing the *Our Son* down the lake, then some twenty miles off Sheboygan, Wisconsin. She had aboard a cargo of pulpwood. Water was rising in the hold. The craft was losing her last battle. Captain Nelson ran up on her mizzenmast the universal distress signal of the seas, the American flag upside down. It snapped out stiffly in the gale. Off toward the horizon the crew could see the outline of a freighter. Was it moving toward them? Would it come close enough to see their signal? After many anxious minutes the men saw the freighter bearing toward them. It had sighted their signal!

OUR SON

Gradually it approached the wallowing *Our Son*. The rescue ship was the *William Nelson* in command of the late Captain Charles Mohr, hero of several lake rescues who was later awarded the Congressional Medal of Honor. He had made out the plight of the old windjammer and had broadcast a wireless message telling of her situation.

Another steamer was also coming to the rescue. It was the carferry *Pere Marquette 22*, with Captain W. H. Van Dyke in charge. He was arriving in answer to the wireless message of the *William Nelson*. Aboard the big carferry a man named Ferris watched the rescue efforts of the *William Nelson* and brought his camera into action. The pictures that he took are shown by lake marine enthusiasts the length of the Great Lakes.

For two hours Captain Mohr maneuvered his big steamer to take off the seven men that comprised the crew of the *Our Son*. Three times he circled the sinking schooner. At last the right moment arrived. After pouring storm oil to break the high seas, Captain Mohr placed the bow of his vessel so that the men on the schooner could climb aboard his ship.

Abandoned on the big lake, the ancient windjammer floated sluggishly, fatally waterlogged, her bare masts weaving with the rolling hull. In an hour she had slowly settled beneath the waves. The last of the grand old fleet of Great Lakes windjammers had gone down "in the harness". Never famous as a calamity ship, but instead admired and loved by the men of the lakes, the *Our Son* rounded out better than a half century of strenuous work in serving the transportation needs of two fast growing neighboring nations.

Chapter Fourteen
THE LOWER LIGHTS

It was one of those pleasant early spring evenings in Florida. The sky was clear, and myriads of stars twinkled, forming a mighty ceiling with nature's own illumination. The mockingbirds chattered softly in the trees. The steady deep booming of the ocean's surf breaking on the hard white sands nearby was all that disturbed the silence. The modest little town of Coronado Beach bathed in this quiet beauty.

A few persons strolled along the main street, sauntering idly. Not a few turned into the rambling building which served as the community club house. Its open windows glowed with soft lights. Inside, a group of middle-aged folks clustered about an ancient grand piano. Prominent among them were four snowy white haired men, robust and hale despite their tell-tale crowning glory.

"Now, Sarah, let's have the 'Lower Lights.' That's our old favorite," said one of them.

"All right, captain. Here goes," replied the smiling pianist.

Her fingers played over the yellowed keys and out of the instrument came softly the beautiful strains of that grand old hymn, "Brightly Beams Our Father's Mercy."

THE LOWER LIGHTS

The four white heads drew close together and arms were placed on each others shoulders as their voices blended with the music. Soon everyone in the room joined in the singing and the strains were wafted out of the open windows into the gorgeous night. The first verse went along smoothly.

"Brightly beams our Father's mercy
From His lighthouse evermore,
But to us He gives the keeping
Of the lights along the shore."

As if to substantiate the verse, the flashing gleam from the tall Ponce De Leon Inlet Lighthouse splashed through the trees. It would flash unfailingly all through that night, as it had done for thousands of other nights, peaceful and stormy, and would continue to do in the years to come. Keepers came and went, but the light never failed. Men far out at sea counted on that glimmer of light and it never let them down.

Then came the rousing chorus. Here the singers did their best, and to the folks on the sidewalk who had gathered to listen it was good to hear. They too joined in, humming.

MEMORIES OF THE LAKES

"Let the lower lights be burning!
Send a gleam across the wave!
Some poor fainting, struggling seaman
You may rescue, you may save."

"Gosh, Bill, that's still a great old song," enthused one of the oldsters. "No one appreciates it like us old sailors, I don't suppose. Fifty years afloat makes a man realize that a lighthouse is his best friend."

This was a pleasant occasion for these four men, each a shipmaster in his own right. Collectively they had spent two centuries sailing ships on the Great Lakes. The cargoes that they had safely transported would build a mountain. Each winter when their lakes were frozen solid they would journey to sunny Florida and there relax until duty again called them back to their bridges.

Coronado's regular townsfolk had come to love these old mariners. They looked forward to their arrival each winter, and regretted their leaving each springtime. The skippers became a part of the life of the town. Their homes were show places, and were decorated with old anchors, capstans, lanterns, flags, and such. Each captain owned his own place, but their most prized possessions were their small boats, rigged with single sail and immaculately kept. Almost every fine day they could be seen tacking and luffing on the broad waters of the nearby inlet.

"Another verse, Sarah, please," one of them begged. So again the music pealed forth, as the second verse commenced.

THE LOWER LIGHTS

"Dark the night of sin has settled,
Loud the angry billows roar;
Eager eyes are watching, longing,
For the lights along the shore."

Again the chorus rang out, and Sarah, knowing that the third verse would be demanded, swung right into it.

"Trim your feeble lamp, my brother:
Some poor sailor tempest-tossed,
Trying now to make the harbor,
In the darkness may be lost."

The last strains died away in that starlight night, and the neighbors who gathered in the clubhouse for the evening had had their entertainment and went their various ways.

The following afternoon the four shipmasters gathered on Captain Bill's lawn and sat there overlooking the inlet, chatting.

"Nice evenin' last night," remarked one.

"Sure was, and we finished up with our old favorite song," replied another.

"Did I ever tell you about the feller that made a trip with me last summer? He had an idea about that song! And I think he might be on the right track," spoke one of the skippers. "It seems as how this song was written by a famous evangelist with a nice name. Bliss, it was, Philip Paul Bliss. He wrote a lot of hymns and such. Had a hankerin' for the water in lots of them. Another one he wrote is that old favorite of so many sailors, 'Pull For The

Shore.' Well, it seems that Mr. Bliss, as I said before, had a hankerin' for the water, and he followed the doin's of the boats very closely, Great Lakes boats, as that was where he lived and worked.

"Well, about 1864, I think it was, when he was a young man, the little port of Cleveland had a shocking marine disaster. It seems that there were two sets of lights marking the harbor at that time, just little old oil lanterns, I suppoz'. One was ashore in the big lighthouse on the hill-top about where those big warehouses are now, but at best it was only a glimmer. Of course it would help a lot when a feller was way out on the lake. It showed him where Cleveland was, anyhow. But that light wasn't a bit of good after you got ready to come inside the harbor proper. It seems there were some stone breakwaters in those days that jutted lakeward and formed a protecting channel at the mouth of the Cuyahoga River.

"All this was almost eighty years ago. Well, sir, an old steamer, with passengers and freight, was caught off Cleveland one wild night that year trying to make port. Her skipper located the high light in the lighthouse but found only one of the lower lights on the pier-heads burning. So in the blackness of the night her skipper had to decide which one of those pier-head lights was not burning. As bad luck was running for the captain that night, he guessed the wrong one and so missed the channel opening and crashed his bows into the pier. The old ship smashed herself into kindling and was a total wreck, so the story goes. He said that quite a few folks aboard lost their lives in the accident.

"The newspapers of the day told of the wreck, and the people along the lakes were shocked to learn that disaster could come to a ship right smack at a harbor entrance like that. Folks were much impressed with what they read and churches held services for the dead.

"Well, this man I am tellin' you about, the one that made the trip with me, he figgers that this chap Bliss likely learned of the shipwreck and was greatly moved by it. Seein' as how he was so boat-minded and all, he sat down and wrote off this fine old hymn. And darned if I don't believe that is how it came to be written."

"Sure does sound likely," thoughtfully mused another of the ancient mariners.

"Sure does," they all agreed.

⚓ ⚓ ⚓ ⚓ ⚓ ⚓ ⚓ ⚓

CHAPTER FIFTEEN

GRACE DARLING

The old adage that history repeats itself is often evident. Many events of ocean navigation of bygone years have been repeated on the fresh water of the Great Lakes. One such incident is that of a daring rescue made by a light-house keeper's daughter.

Over a century ago, in September 1838, all Britain thrilled to the tale of Grace Darling, the frail, twenty-two year old daughter of the keeper of the Longstone Light on the Farne Islands. The ship *Forfarshire,* bound from an English port to Scotland, was wrecked within sight of their lighthouse.

Grace Darling and her father, William, rowed their heavy surf boat through tempestuous seas and in several trips brought back to the lighthouse the nine persons they found clinging to the sea swept rocks.

All England acclaimed the wisp of a girl as a heroine. Queen Victoria, newly crowned, learning of the rescue, invited the light-keeper and his daughter to the Royal Court and there presented each with a gold medal. Their rescue boat is said to be preserved to this day. Grace Darling lived but four years after her famous rescue, but her name and memory has survived in the minds of England's seafaring men for over a hundred years.

166

GRACE DARLING

Nearly forgotten is the equally heroic counterpart story of pretty Maebelle Mason, daughter of Captain and Mrs. Orlo J. Mason. Captain Mason was the keeper of the Mamajuda Island Light in the Lower Detroit River. He lived with his wife and their fourteen year old daughter on the tiny, oddly named island on which the light was built.

On the morning of May 11th, 1890, Captain Mason went to the mainland for supplies, leaving his wife and daughter alone at the lighthouse. Their only means of transportation, since the captain had taken their main boat, was a small flat-bottomed skiff that lay high on the tiny island beach.

Maebelle and her mother noted the approach of the big freighter, *C. W. Elphicke,* downbound for Lake Erie. It came close to the light. The captain, megaphone in hand, leaned over his bridge rail and shouted the astonishing news that a man was struggling in the water with his over-turned and sinking row boat about a mile upstream. It was impossible for him to stop the heavily laden freighter in the strong current and attempt to rescue the unfortunate individual. So the captain did the next best thing by reporting it to the lighthouse, little expecting that it was manned only by a woman and a girl.

Face to face with the responsibility, the two dragged their only boat into the water. Maebelle insisted that she go alone after the man. The strong current was bringing the sinking row boat with the man still clinging to it nearer the light. Maebelle knew that, if he swirled past

167

her, she would likely never be able to catch him. It was then or never. The man's life hung in the balance. The young girl pulled with all her might on the skiff's oars. She intercepted the fastly drifting wreck almost abreast of the lighthouse. It was both difficult and dangerous to haul the almost unconscious man into her little boat, but she tugged at his clothing and somehow managed to get him safely into her skiff. She headed back for the light and after a hard row, deftly landed the skiff with its half-drowned occupant on the little beach. The mother and daughter then set about reviving their exhausted visitor. By the time Captain Mason returned he was resting comfortably.

The story of her rescue spread rapidly, and Maebelle Mason soon found herself in the role of a heroine. Detroit and Cleveland newspapers told of her valiant deed. The marine magazines of the day also carried the tale.

At a big celebration in Detroit she was awarded a United States Life Saving Medal. The appreciative Shipmasters' Association also presented her with a gold life saving medal. For a long time afterwards the skippers saluted the little heroine when their ships would pass Mamajuda Light.

Fortunately, the life story of Maebelle Mason did not parallel that of her heroine predecessor, Grace Darling. Maebelle eventually married and left her island home and is reported living a long and happy life.

⚓ ⚓ ⚓ ⚓ ⚓ ⚓ ⚓ ⚓

CHAPTER SIXTEEN

YESTERYEARS

The heyday of the Great Lakes passenger steamboat is past. True, glittering luxury lake liners still plough the fresh water of the inland seas, but the old dependable plodding port-to-port steamer has almost vanished into the realms of yesteryear. No longer do these ships crowd the larger terminal lake ports to load all sorts of deck freight to be floated to the smaller ports which depended upon these shipments for their livelihood. No longer do husky Irish stevedores sweat and strain with the loading of such merchandise, while heavily-mustached gentlemen and long-skirted lady passengers shuffle shoreward.

There existed a definite charm about these now vanished ships. Their pleasant deep-throated whistles brought a thrill to all who heard them. Each of these steamboats was distinctive and had its own admirable qualities. The men who sailed them were venturous souls and were well respected in all the ports at which their craft called. To the staid townsmen these seafarers represented the outside world. They were their contact with this great beyond.

No lover of things marine will ever forget going aboard one of these old vessels. The main cabin or saloon was usually entered directly from the gangplank. There, in tiny box-like enclosures, were the purser's and steward's offices. Elegant hand carved woodwork adorned the public rooms. Crews had the time to shine the many brass embellishments that decorated the cabins and decks, and the owners could afford to keep them shined.

Freight was carried on the main deck usually forward of the passengers' saloon and was brought aboard over a separate gangway. There on the freight deck was the delightful aroma of new rope and creosote, and up from a deep dark grated hole in the deck came the musical clanking of hard steel shovels on the iron rim of the fire door.

The ship's engine room, usually on the main deck amidships, was a sight to behold. Passengers looking in the open doorway marvelled at the immaculate machinery. Not a smudge of dirt anywhere! Bright steel levers and ponderous pistons stood waiting for the hands of the engineer to start them into powerful rythmical action.

When sailing time came most of the roustabouts rested and came to the rail, as did the passengers on the upper deck, to watch the ship slip gracefully away from the dock. Bells clanged in the engine room, and the whistle sounded over the waterfront as black velvety smoke rolled upward into the clear blue heavens; the still water was churned into frenzied white foam as the paddle wheels revolved and the walking beam began its ceaseless up-and-down movement.

Large flags broke out in the breeze from the many staffs rising from the hurricane deck. The Jack was always at the bow, and the Stars and Stripes, or the Flag of Canada, at the stern; the house-flag at the mainmast truck, and almost any kind of a banner in between. Many steamboats flew large flags bearing their own names, along with others carrying the names of the ports to which they traded. Not uncommon on the later steamers was the skipper's blue pennant of the Shipmasters' Association with his membership number in large white figures. The men of the lakes loved large flags.

Thus was the old sidewheeler off to the next port, sometimes only a few minutes distant and sometimes several days away. In this manner were the lake cities served in bygone days.

Modern transportation has done away with the old time Great Lakes passenger steamer. They could not survive the competition of today. One by one the ships grew old, wore out, and were dismantled. Operating companies failed or quit. Today not a walking beam steamer plies the Great Lakes where at one time scores sailed from the larger ports.

Not all the old time steamboats of the lakes were sidewheelers; many were propellers. These vessels were a bit less romantic in their sailing than were the sidewheelers, probably due to the fact that they created less commotion in the water in getting under way from a dock.

The early lake steamers, sidewheelers and propellers alike, had quaint pilot houses, usually octagonal in shape, although many had but six sides. Their windows were of intricate design, some having many small panes in odd shapes. Many early steamers had an ungainly set of steps with a pipe railing that led to a small platform atop the pilot house, where the skipper would stand and direct the ship's movements.

Also atop the pilot house was usually a fancy carved ornament depicting something pertaining to the vessel. Sometimes it would be the name of the ship worked into a statue, as in the case of the steamers *India, China* and *Japan,* each of which carried a life-size statue of a native Indian, Chinese and Japanese. Huge carved eagles with great wing spread were popular; while some preferred the falcon with its ferocious look; many others had a sleek horse in various stages of speed. One freighter, the *William Edwards,* carried the life-size bust of its namesake atop its pilot house. The *Fred S. Pabst,* another freighter, had beer kegs at her mastheads.

Ornate woodwork, both on deck and inside, marked the early steamers. Builders apparently had more time in those days for such decorations and embellishments, and owners more money to pay for their installation and up-keep. Today the trend is exactly the opposite; to have no bric-a-brac and to streamline wherever possible.

Nightfall presented a picturesque setting aboard the old passenger steamers. Oil lamps furnished their artificial light—interesting old lamps that today would cause a collector of such items to shout with joy, were he fortunate enough to locate one. These were usually of brass and would swing level on a gimbal regardless of the pitch of the ship. They presented no small problem to the cabin boys each morning when it became necessary to shine, re-fuel, and trim each of them. Some ships had as many as a hundred; some more. Outside on deck there were no lights except the usual running lights and masthead lanterns required by law for navigation purposes. The invention of the electric light was a welcome innovation aboard ship.

Here and there along the Great Lakes shores are lovers of the bygone splender of the all but forgotten passenger steamers. These men have collected, usually from the unsentimental wreckers, bits of interesting parts of the ships themselves. Here is a man who greatly prizes the old bell from the steamer *Idlewild*, the *City of Erie*, the *Tashmoo*, the *Goodtime*, or almost any steamer dear to his memory; there is a man who cherishes a beautifully carved and inlaid wood steering wheel of a famous old lake liner. Collectors hold them priceless.

Even the steam whistles of popular ships are held in great esteem by the lake fans. One such collector in Bedford, Ohio, has mounted on his building the whistle from the old passenger steamer *City of Buffalo*, and has connected it with compressed air. Without fail every noon the residents of Bedford hear the old whistle that was so much a part of that old lake ship. In a display room in the same building he has mounted the steering wheel and other navigating instruments from the *City of Buffalo*. A man who operates a nursery near Newark, Ohio, has mounted the whistle of the old steamer *Chippewa* atop his boiler house, from where it regularly sends its deep rich tone throughout the countryside.

Many men in the lake cities have taken up the enchanting hobby of collecting photographs of lake vessels. They also collect bits of interesting history about the various ships. Hundreds of mementoes of bygone ships of the lakes are cherished in the homes that line the shores. Perhaps it is a maritime lantern, or it may be an ancient anchor, a capstan, a propeller, or most any part of a ship that has been gathered by a man or woman interested in things marine.

The excellent Edison Museum in Dearborn, Michigan, founded and maintained by Mr. Henry Ford, has a great many very interesting parts of old lake ships, mostly engines, some complete and ready to operate. Many large historical societies of long standing throughout the Lakes Country value their vessel collections as priceless. Some have valuable models depicting both the old and the new types of lake shipping.

Local steamship and marine historical societies are being formed to gather and preserve the almost forgotten lore of the early Great Lakes shipping. Much credit is due these folks who, without thought of profit to themselves and purely as a hobby, are preserving for posterity that part of the history of our great country.

Old timers looking lakeward over the clear sparkling waters like to think back to the days of the old ships. With half-closed eyes they fancy a smoke smudge on the horizon to be the old *Idlewild* or possibly the *Metropolis* returning, which in reality is one of the many great bulk carriers floating thousands of tons of iron ore down the old historic lake waterway. They have taken over where the old side-wheelers left off.

⚓ ⚓ ⚓ ⚓ ⚓ ⚓ ⚓ ⚓

Chapter Seventeen

TOUGH DAYS

The white-haired oldsters of the Great Lakes often re-call those earlier days of windjammer sailing, when time in port was long. Both the loading and unloading of schooners in those days were done by manual labor. Shovels, buckets, wheelbarrows and mules were the prin-cipal tools of the rough stevedores when iron ore and coal were first floated up and down the Great Lakes. The work was hard and the play was also hard. The law was indif-ferent and seldom interfered. Ship captains ruled largely by sheer strength, courage and ability.

Rough and tough men and women lived in and con-trolled the waterfronts of the lake ports, both upper and lower. Each port had its notorious strong men in the shipping world, and each skipper of a ship had his reputa-tion for being a hard individual.

Sailors hesitated to go ashore alone after nightfall for fear of being beaten and robbed. The mushroom growth of the brothels paralleled the mushroom growth of the schooner trade on the lakes. Immoral houses flourished. Saloons were rough, and daily fights prevailed. One notorious saloon-keeper at a lower lake port had a crafty idea to keep business in his emporium at peak demand. On rare occasions when the barroom would get quiet, he

175

would step to his doorway, revolver in hand, and shoot several times into the air. Soon there would be a rush of nearby men to the spot to see what was happening, not wishing to miss a good fight. The owner would pass the shooting off lightly. The disappointed new arrivals, once in the saloon, usually turned to some drinking, and business momentarily picked up in the barroom.

One old windjammer skipper recalls that five separate murders occured in one of the lower lake ports on one occasion when he was unloading an ore cargo there.

Law and order gradually caught up with the lawlessness. Equally hard and determined men set about to clean up the waterfronts, and by the time the steel freighter nosed her way into these ports the tough joints and brothels had almost vanished.

The lake schooner sailor however had a rough shore existence at both ends of the trip. The northern ports, where copper, iron ore and lumber were stowed aboard, were equally as tough as were the unloading ports, but in a cruder manner. Plain skullduggery was practiced on the iron ranges and the loading docks, with no finesse. Plenty of deceit and fraud entered into the southern unloading ports, but the northern lumber-jacks and ore "rasslers" knew little of cunning.

The ancient art of shanghaiing was practiced on the lakes in those days. Not unfrequently an adventurous sailor with pay in his pockets would go ashore and fall into the clutches of the gamblers, women and men, in the joints. Unable to locate him at sailing time, his ship would leave without him. Some time later the luckless sailor might regain consciousness to find himself penniless, bruised and cut, aboard another sailing vessel, outbound and rolling under the swells of a reviving lake breeze.

Whole crews would sometimes go ashore together for safety and would likely get thoroughly drunk and eventually return to their ship in a high state of exhilaration. This was usually under the cover of darkness. A feeble oil lantern would be doing its utmost to illuminate the forecastle. The procedure on such an occasion would be for one of the crew to vigorously throw his boot at the offending light, promptly putting it out. Then a rousing shout, "Every man for himself for fifteen minutes," would be the signal for a good rough and tumble fight in the darkness of the forecastle. Such were the ideas of these sailors of a good time. Then would come the husky ship's mate and put an end to the skirmish. Those mates were a hard set of men and part of their duty was to keep order aboard ship.

Story has it that the mate of the big five-masted schooner *David Dows*, a strapping six footer and a champion "collar bone and elbow" wrestler of the time, once stepped into a forecastle free-for-all battle. Spitting on his hands as he entered the melee in the darkness, and grabbing the nearest man, he tossed him bodily out through the doorway onto the deck. Another and another followed until the room was clear of men. The mate adjusted his clothing and returned to his other duties. A pile of unkempt, disheveled, and badly bruised humanity untangled itself on the deck. The crew, by then a more sober lot, crawled back into their bunks to sleep off their hilarity and heal their bruises. Yes, indeed, the early lake sailors were a hardy lot!

Chapter Eighteen

THE FRIDAY SHIP

One of the most foreboding of sailor omens is the Friday one. They believe that nothing should be started on a Friday, if any good is expected to come of it. Many modern freighter captains have been known to find some small work to be done before beginning the sailing season, if on a Friday, that will delay the ship until after midnight, to avoid sailing on that bad luck day.

Not so with the "omen-to-hell" Captain R. A. Seymour, of Manitowoc, Wisconsin, back in 1888. In the old Burger and Burger shipyards there, they were given the order to build a new passenger and freight steamer for him.

"Lay her keel on Friday," instructed Captain Seymour. The omen-fearing ship carpenters were aghast! Such daredevilment was certainly foolhardy, and no good would ever come of it! But the stout keel of the good ship *Petoskey* was laid on a Friday, come good luck or bad. Built of wood, the *Petoskey* had a length of one hundred seventy-one feet, breadth of thirty feet, depth of twelve feet, and tonnage of seven hundred seventy.

Another new and radical departure in her building was that she was one of the first of the steamers to be built without the great overhead arches, so prominent in the steamers of those days. The arches, put there to

179

strengthen the long boats, were considered by Captain Seymour as not necessary in the *Petoskey*. Instead he had her hull diagonally strapped with iron braces.

In due time the builders had the *Petoskey* ready for launching, and a neat craft she was.

"Put her in on a Friday," again ordered Captain Seymour.

Now the seafaring men of Lake Michigan were certain that something awful would happen to a ship with such a start. It was not good to tempt the devil too far.

But the *Petoskey* was launched on a Friday with as perfect a job as could be wished for.

The next omen-be-damned came when Captain Seymour ordered her to start on her maiden voyage on a Friday. That really required courage! But it was on a Friday that the new and trim steamer *Petoskey* sailed past the Manitowoc harbor lights and out onto Lake Michigan on her first trip.

The ship entered the Chicago, Traverse City and Petoskey run and all went well. The old timers were astounded. Bad lake storms came and went and the sturdy *Petoskey* took them all in her stride. Sometimes ships were lost in those storms, but not the Friday Ship. Years slipped by, ten—twenty—thirty—even forty, and still nothing direfull happened to the *Petoskey,* not a major mishap!

The vessel rounded out almost a half century in good and faithful service on Lake Michigan before coming to a peaceful end. The Friday bad omen had been severly tested and found wanting.

⚓ ⚓ ⚓ ⚓ ⚓ ⚓ ⚓ ⚓

CHAPTER NINETEEN

THE WHALEBACKS

The forty-six year old steamer *Alexander McDougall* sidled up to a long unloading dock on the lower lakes one day in the summer of 1944 and her skipper, Captain John Mier, directed the job of making her fast. Immediately the giant Huletts were at work taking from her hold the heavy red iron ore which she had floated down from the northland of Minnesota. The historic old ship had completed another successful voyage. It would be almost impossible to figure exactly just how many successful cargoes the *Alexander McDougall* had delivered. Trip after trip, through fair weather and foul, the old whaleback hauled iron ore, coal, grain, stone, and kindred cargoes safely to their destinations on the Great Lakes.

"She isn't just exactly the same as the other whalebacks," explained Captain Mier. "Her bow is standard, while the other whalebacks had a bow that sort of came to a blunt point on a line with the deck, like a pig's nose. All the old timers still call them pigs. Only three of the whaleback steamers are left now, the *John Ericsson*, the tanker *Meteor*, and us, and a few of the barges. And we are due to be scrapped at the end of the war," he added a bit sadly.

Elements of romance and tragedy are woven into the tale of the whaleback ships that are so nearly gone from

181

the Great Lakes. They are a type of ship that belongs almost entirely to the Great Lakes. Conceived by a Great Lakes skipper, built on the Great Lakes, sailed on the Great Lakes, with most of them ending their days on the Great Lakes, they are truly a symbol of Great Lakes ingenuity. Several whalebacks found their way to salt water, and in some out-of-the-way spot on the seven seas may still be freighting cargoes. A few were built on salt water. They were all good ships in their day, but like the canals and the interurban electric cars, they became out-moded. Old age, difficulty in unloading, and smallness of cargo, were the principal objections.

In all there were about forty of these ships constructed on the lakes. Fourteen of them were steamers and the rest barges. When without cargo they float on the water like a cigar, with their living quarters and engine room perched on the stern. When fully loaded, the whalebacks settled into the water so that their decks would be but seven or eight feet above the water's surface. Often the waves would wash over their main deck. They were designed to offer minimum resistance to wind and sea.

Only one passenger ship of the whaleback type was built, the *Christopher Columbus*. Constructed in 1892 and put in commission the following year on the six mile run between Chicago and the World's Fair then in progress at Jackson Park, this ship proved exceedingly popular. After the Fair she operated on the Chicago and Milwaukee day run for the Goodrich Line. Undoubtedly the *Christopher Columbus* did more than any of the other whalebacks to focus attention on that particular type of vessel, as it is claimed that she carried more passengers during her lifetime than any other lake ship. After forty-four years afloat, the *Christopher Columbus* was dismantled in Manitowoc, Wisconsin.

The whaleback was designed, patented, and built by Captain Alexander McDougall, a Scotchman, who had migrated as a boy to Canada, and like so many of his countrymen, had turned to the water for his livelihood. In 1864 he began sailing on the Great Lakes. Eventually he became a master of vessels. At one time he was captain of the steamer *Japan,* an early and successful passenger boat plying between Buffalo and Duluth. In 1872 he conceived the idea of the monitor type of ship with the odd shaped hull, better known later as the whaleback. From that time his activities were concentrated largely on the promotion and development of his new type of ship. It was promptly dubbed "McDougall's Dream" by some of the wags of the waterfront.

By hard work and careful management Captain McDougall managed to construct his first barge. He gave it the unromantic name—number *101*. It splashed down the ways at Duluth, Minnesota, on June 23, 1888. It was of about fifteen hundred tons burden, one hundred eighty-seven feet long, twenty-five feet beam, and eighteen feet three inches depth. Two turrets eight feet in diameter and seven feet high were located on her deck, one in the bow and the other in the stern. Through these turrets went the steering gear and towing gear, and other equipment necessary to operate the barge. The whole deck was clear, with hatches for cargo stowage. A pilot house ten feet by twelve feet was placed on the after turret to house the navigators and wheelsman. It is reported to have cost about forty thousand dollars to build.

The *101* was a good start for Captain McDougall, and he used it to demonstrate his ideas. The Rockefeller interests were looking towards the Great Lakes and saw things in McDougall's Dream that interested them. Soon the shore line of West Superior, near Duluth, began to ring with the blows of the riveters' hammers. Barges at first, and then steamers, slid sideways into St. Louis Bay. Nine ships were launched in 1889 and 1890, and nine more were built in 1891. The balance of the whalebacks were constructed from then until July 1898, when Captain McDougall's daughter christened the last of the whalebacks and gave it the name of her father.

The tales of the salt water experiences of the McDougall whalebacks would fill a book. Several of them were taken to the east coast. One, the *Charles W. Wetmore,* crossed the Atlantic with wheat for Liverpool, returned and loaded at New York for Everett, Washington. She sailed around the much dreaded Cape Horn safely to her destination.

Captain McDougall, at the height of the whaleback era, in 1895, was quoted in a San Francisco newspaper as saying, "We have them (whalebacks) on the lakes, on the Atlantic, also a line running on the coast from New York to Tampico; one is now crossing from England, where she was built on contract, and we have one here, with others to be built at Everett, Washington." Some returned to the lakes after their jobs on salt water were completed.

THE WHALEBACKS

While the shapes of the whalebacks were all alike, their dimensions differed. The *Henry Cort,* which came out as the *Pillsbury,* was three hundred twenty feet long, forty-two feet beam, twenty-five feet depth, and a capacity of three thousand five hundred tons, while the *Frank Rockefeller,* later the *South Park,* and now the tanker *Meteor,* is three hundred sixty-six feet long, forty-five feet beam, and twenty-six feet depth, with a capacity of five thousand two hundred tons. The *Alexander Holley,* a barge, is listed as three hundred sixty-one feet keel length, forty-six feet beam, twenty-six feet depth, and six thousand three hundred tons capacity.

Some of the whalebacks finished their careers, as all sailors like to see, by being dismantled, as did the *J. T. Reid,* formerly the *J. B. Neilson,* and originally the *Washburn.* However, the *Clifton,* formerly the *Samual Mather,* was lost in 1924 with all hands on Lake Huron. The *Henry Cort* was wrecked on the breakwall of a Lake Michigan port. The *James B. Colgate* foundered in the Black Friday Storm on Lake Erie on October 16, 1916. Thus the whalebacks have ended their days, some by fair means, and some by foul.

Among the early whalebacks launched at the head of the lakes were: the *Colgate Hoyt, Joseph L. Colby, Charles W. Wetmore, E. B. Bartlett, A. D. Thompson, Thomas Wilson, Samuel Mather, Washburn, Pillsbury, Christopher Columbus,* and others. The steamers *Choctaw* and *Andaste* were of the monitor type of vessel, but were built in Cleveland, in 1892. Some of the barges built by Captain McDougall, and in his connection with The American

Steel Barge Company, at Duluth and Superior were: the 101, 102, 103, 104, 105, 107, 109, 110, 111, 115, 116, 117, 118, 126, 127, 129, 130, 131, 132, 134, 137, 139, 140, 201 and 202.

As these vessels without power changed ownership, the numbered names were usually dropped and other names used, for instance: the 127 became the *Ivie;* the 111, the *Jennie;* the 202, the *Fannie;* the 201, the *Cassie;* the 116, the *Brittania;* the 107, the *Bombay;* the 110, the *Badger;* and so it went. The steamers also had many changes of names, for instance, the *J. B. Trevor*, sold to Canadian owners, became the *Atikokan;* the *Colgate Hoyt* became the *Bay City;* the *E. B. Bartlett* became the *Bay Port;* the *Joseph L. Colby* became the *Bay State;* and the *A. D. Thompson* became the *Bay View.*

It fell to the lot of the whaleback barge 102 to haul the first cargo of Mesabi Range iron ore to Cleveland. She loaded on November 11, 1892 at Superior, Wisconsin, her cargo of two thousand seventy-three tons. Her skipper was Captain E. Peabody. The cargo was arranged by Oglebay, Norton and Company for the Rockefeller interests. The original bill of lading for this memorable cargo is now at the Western Reserve Historical Society in Cleveland.

The rugged and hard-working Scotch navigator who conceived the idea of the whalebacks also left his stamp on many successful lake-head enterprises. Harbor improvements, safer navigation of ships, anything that improved transportation by water, was of vital concern to Captain Alexander McDougall. He passed away in Duluth on May

THE WHALEBACKS

22, 1923, concluding a life of great activity and achievement.

"McDougall's Dream" has safely and economically moved millions of tons of cargo. Exactly when the last of the dream ends will likely never be widely known.

LIST OF WHALEBACKS BUILT ON THE GREAT LAKES

Vessel	No.	Launched	First Load
*Barge	101	June 23, 1888	Two Harbors, ore
*Barge	102	July 17, 1889	Ashland, ore
*Barge	103	Oct. 5, 1889	Duluth, wheat
*Barge	104	Feb. 6, 1890	Two Harbors, ore
*Barge	105	Apr. 22, 1890	Ashland, ore
*Colgate Hoyt	106	June 9, 1890	Ashland, ore
*Barge	107	Aug. 16, 1890	Ashland, ore
Joseph L. Colby	108	Nov. 15, 1890	Superior, wheat
Barge	109	Nov. 15, 1890	Superior, wheat
Barge	110	Apr. 28, 1891	Superior, wheat
Barge	111	Apr. 28, 1891	Superior, wheat
Charles B. Wetmore	112	May 23, 1891	Duluth, wheat
E. B. Bartlett	113	July 9, 1891	Duluth, wheat
A. D. Thompson	114	June 6, 1891	Superior, wheat
Barge	115	Aug. 15, 1891	Superior, wheat
Barge	116	Aug. 29, 1891	Superior, wheat
Barge	117	Nov. 14, 1891	Duluth, wheat
Barge	118	Dec. 5, 1891	Duluth, wheat
Thomas Wilson	119	Apr. 30, 1892	Duluth, wheat
Samuel Mather	120	May 21, 1892	Two Harbors, ore
James B. Colgate	121	Sept. 21, 1892	Superior, wheat
Sagamore (barge)	122	July 23, 1892	Two Harbors, ore
Pathfinder	123	July 16, 1892	Two Harbors, ore
Washburn	124	June 25, 1892	Superior, wheat
Pillsbury	125	June 25, 1892	Duluth and Superior
Barge	126	Dec. 17, 1892	Superior, wheat
Barge	127	Oct. 29, 1892	Duluth, flour
Christopher Columbus	128	Dec. 3, 1892	Passengers (5,600)
Barge	129	May 13, 1893	Superior, wheat
Barge	130	May 27, 1893	Superior, wheat
Barge	131	June 3, 1893	Superior, wheat
Barge	132	June 17, 1893	Duluth, wheat
Barge	134	June 10, 1893	Duluth, wheat
John B. Trevor	135	May 1, 1895	Mesabi, ore
Frank Rockefeller	136	Apr. 25, 1896	Mesabi, ore
Barge	137	May 9, 1896	Mesabi, ore
John Ericsson	138	July 11, 1896	Ashland, ore
Barge	139	Aug. 12, 1896	Mesabi, ore
Barge	140	Apr. 21, 1897	Ashland, ore
Barge	201	Apr. 30, 1897	
Barge	202	Apr. 30, 1897	
Alexander McDougall		July, 1898	(Modified bow)

*These vessels were built at Duluth. The others listed were built at Superior.

187

⚓ ⚓ ⚓ ⚓ ⚓ ⚓ ⚓ ⚓

CHAPTER TWENTY

THE MARY CELESTE

The *Mary Celeste* was not a Great Lakes vessel. Instead she plowed the salty oceans. Built in Nova Scotia, on the Bay of Fundy, in 1861, the year that the Civil War began in the United States, the *Mary Celeste* (launched as the *Amazon*) was little different from dozens of sailing vessels then on the Great Lakes. She was classed as a "half-brig" and had two masts, the foremast being square-rigged, and the mainmast, fore-and-aft or schooner-rigged. Her latest recorded measurements were: length 103 feet, breadth 25.7 feet, depth 16.2 feet, and total tonnage of 282.28 tons.

To the *Mary Celeste* fell the lot of being one of the most talked-of ships in the world. Sailing alone without captain or crew, she was found by the British brigantine *Dei Gratia* on the afternoon of Wednesday, December 4th, 1872, on the high seas between the Azores and the coast of Portugal. There have been other ships similarly found upon the high seas but none have had the notoriety that has been accorded the *Mary Celeste*. The mystery has never been solved.

The *Dei Gratia* had sailed from New York on the 15th of November, 1872, exactly eight days after the *Mary Celeste* had left that same port. The *Mary Celeste* had a cargo of alcohol in casks and was bound for Genoa, Italy.

THE MARY CELESTE

The *Dei Gratia* carried petroleum and was bound for Gibraltar. The two vessels therefore sailed practically the same course. The eight men comprising the crew of the *Mary Celeste,* including the master, had completely vanished. The captain's wife and two-year-old daughter had also disappeared. The derelict vessel was in sound condition, as was her cargo, part of her sails were set and, except for small damage likely to occur on any long voyage, the ship was in good condition. Entries in her log ended on Monday, November 25th, 1872. They were ordinary marine notations and cast no light on her forthcoming mystery. The abandoned ship was sailed into Gibraltar by men of the crew of the *Dei Gratia* and the world then learned of the strange finding of the *Mary Celeste.*

Investigation after investigation occurred but nothing except theory resulted. Sailormen all over the world expressed their ideas but no one knew for sure what had happened aboard the *Mary Celeste.* Much has been written and much has been discussed about the little sailing vessel, but to this day, almost seventy-five years later, the *Mary Celeste* story is still as much a mystery as ever.

The Great Lakes have had their counterparts of the *Mary Celeste* story. There was the schooner *Maud S.* that was found on Lake Ontario making her eerie way alone toward the Welland Canal. There was also the schooner *Lithophone* that was sighted by the passenger steamer *Lakeside* late one afternoon as she wallowed her way alone in western Lake Ontario. Too, there is the tale of the lumber steamer *Eliza H. Strong* that was found on Lake Superior with her stack and part of her cabins gone and her deck cargo awry, but with never a soul aboard to explain the weird circumstance. There is a real fascination about a ship found sailing the waters minus the humans that made up her crew. It is a challange to the keenest and most observing minds to calculate the reasons or causes.

The explanation is usually simple, in spite of the mysterious surroundings. In the cases of the lonely ships of the lakes, their tales have been pieced together and are here related.

In the quaint Canadian harbor of Port Credit, Ontario, in the early spring of 1899, lay the sturdy sailing schooner *Maud S.* She was a bit different from the other vessels plying the ancient trade of stone hauling along the north shore of Lake Ontario in that she had a forefoot. Old timers accounted for this finery in a craft of such humble calling by explaining that, when she was built in 1884, her builders used the keel, stem, forefoot, and sternpost of the former yacht *Geraldine,* of the famous Gooderham fleet. The *Geraldine* had been left to decay in Port Credit harbor, but her main members, with some strengthening, could still be made strong and useful. Thus the modest little schooner was built around the bones of the comely yacht.

Inspiringly she was named after that famous horse, the racing trotter, Maud S. And as for being trim, the namesake boat was all that could be expected of her. Sailormen termed her "a smart and handy craft"—which is a good recommendation in sailor talk.

THE MARY CELESTE

So it was that she lay in the little river that forms the harbor of Port Credit. One night she was at her dock with everything shipshape. The next morning she was gone! Shortly after daybreak it was discovered the *Maud S.* was missing. Owners and harbormen were astounded. Where could the schooner be? The vast expanses of Lake Ontario held no clue. Not a thing could be seen floating on its cold waters. The *Maud S.* had surely disappeared.

Many theories were advanced, such as pirates, scuttling, and the like, but her owner discounted all. Logically he reasoned that his craft had slipped her mooring and had drifted out on the lake. Her anchor chain which had been made fast ashore to a post had parted, leaving a piece of it still around the mooring post, and her other lines, apparently unable to stand the additional strain, had also parted. He noted that the wind was from the northwest and was blowing strong. His ship would go before that wind and must be out there somewhere. She was staunch and sound and could easily withstand the sea that was running. He knew that she would still be afloat.

The ice in Credit River had broken up just before the *Maud S.* took to her nautical heels, and the freshet that followed the ice jam evidently made sufficient current to part a weak link in her anchor chain, which facts probably accounted for the unheralded departure of the little schooner.

Across the lake in the direction that the wind would carry her, lay the entrance to the Wellend Canal, Port Dalhousie. It was almost thirty miles across. There tugs

191

were available to search for the odd runaway. Her owner hurried by train to that port and obtained the services of such a craft.

As they approached the big lake they spied the schooner sailing along serenely all by herself some seven miles off shore. The busy tug chugged along after the miscreant and upon overtaking her, a line was made fast to her bow and she was forthwith brought to dock. Subsequent inspection proved that she was not the least injured by her nocturnal escapade and she had not shipped a drop of water. The *Maud S.* proved that she was a good sailor, slipping unseen past other vessels moored in the harbor and out upon the broad waters of Lake Ontario, with not a soul aboard! No hand upon her wheel to guide her destiny!

Another itinerant windjammer of Lake Ontario that sallied forth upon its chilly waters one early spring evening was the schooner *Lithophone.* Not a living sound could be heard within her cabin or on her deck that night; her captain and crew were ashore in their homes. Notwithstanding, the ship quietly parted her lines and slowly swung away from her dock as neatly as though her crew were in their accustomed places. Down the short stream that makes the harbor she sailed, and out upon the wide waters of Lake Ontario. A cruise to where?

When daylight came it was discovered that the *Lithophone* was missing from her moorings. Four hardy sailors set out in the penetrating cold of early morning in the fishing smack *Hecla* with the hope of locating the wandering *Lithophone*. During the night fresh sheet ice had formed on the surface of Lake Ontario. The men found it necessary to stand in the bow of the *Helca* and break the ice with poles and oars lest its sharp edges cut through the thin planking of the smack.

All day they searched the lake for signs of the *Lithophone* but always she was just over the horizon or hidden from view by the mists—for never a glimpse of the wandering ship did they obtain. Chilled to the bones they put into Port Dalhousie, Ontario, across the lake from their starting port to get rest and help. They intended to hire a steam tug and to continue the search the next day.

But that evening a small passenger steamer, *Lakeside*, under command of Captain Wigal, arrived in Port Dalhousie from Toronto and reported sighting the lonely *Lithophone* sailing her uncharted course out on the open lake. The captain told the searchers where he had last seen the windjammer. So, with that wisp of hope, they set out again on the following morning to continue their search.

Hours passed as the *Hecla* sailed a zigzag course, hoping to sight the *Lithophone*. Shortly after noon their efforts were rewarded. There, low in the water, in the chill mist that covered the lake, lay the *Lithophone*. Her decks were awash. A few more hours out there alone and she would most likely have found the bottom of the lake.

The *Hecla* was run alongside and pumps started on the

Lithophone and by much hard labor she was freed of her surplus water. Otherwise she was uninjured. She made port that night and a tired crew made certain that the wandering windjammer was made fast.

Darkness was settling over Lake Superior on August 30, 1901, when the lumber-laden steamer *Mueller* sighted the steamer *Eliza H. Strong,* another lumber-laden craft. The after deck house and stack of the *Eliza H. Strong* were missing, and part of her deck cargo was gone. The weather was ordinary. The *Mueller* went closer to investigate and offer help. Not a person could be seen aboard the *Eliza H. Strong!*

The mate and two seamen from the *Mueller* boarded the lonely *Strong.* They made a line fast between the two ships and altered the course of the *Mueller.* With the *Strong* thus in tow they headed for Munising, Michigan. Imagine their surprise upon reaching that harbor entrance the following morning to find the captain and crew of the *Strong* aboard a tug bound for the open lake to rescue their damaged vessel.

It developed that the *Eliza H. Strong,* with the schooner *Commodore* in tow, bound from Duluth to Buffalo, had sprung a leak which could not be stopped and which eventually extingushed the fires under her boilers. A list developed and caused part of her deck cargo of lumber to shift. In going overboard it carried away the after cabins and smoke stack. The entire crew left the *Strong* and boarded the *Commodore,* sailing her into Munising to get a tug to bring in their disabled steamer.

A very interesting salvage case developed from this situation and eventually reached the United States District Court in Grand Rapids, Michigan. The men on the *Mueller* claimed salvage on the *Strong.* The *Strong* defended by claiming that their ship was not a derelict, and that they were about to retrieve her when the *Mueller* hove in sight. The Court decided to allow the crew of the *Mueller* some remuneration for their services, but not anything like the expected reward.

After considerable litigation the *Strong* was returned to her owners. She was re-conditioned and again sailed the lakes in the lumber trade. She was no longer considered a ship of mystery. Mystery ceases to be a lure when explained.

True, these lake counterparts of the *Mary Celeste* lack the mystery that surrounds this latter ship, but is it not likely that whatever caused the *Mary Celeste* to sail along alone might not have been as simple in explanation if it were but told? It is the uncertainty of what caused the vessel's plight that adds the thrill of mystery and consequent interest in the case.

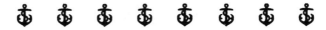

Chapter Twenty-One

THE FLYER OF THE LAKES

An islander always admires a ship. He also carries an utmost respect for a ship and usually for the men who sail them. So it is with the islanders that live permanently, and the vacationists too, on the dozen or more spots of land that dot the shimmering waters of western Lake Erie.

They, one and all, held the passenger and freight steamer *Frank E. Kirby* in greatest esteem. Did she not bring them their supplies—food, clothing and shelter? She hauled away their produce and carried their mail. She took away those who left the islands for other fields and occasionally would return them in their caskets, to be buried forever on their island. For twenty-nine years the *Frank E. Kirby* served those islands faithfully. Children were born within the sound of her whistle, lived and grew up within its sonorous tone, played on the beaches and were married in the islands' churches. Small wonder that the ship that brought them their contact with the outside world was loved so by these island folk. To the city dwellers of Detroit and Sandusky, her terminals, the ship proved to be a source of pleasure, relaxation and enjoyment. A trip on the *Frank E. Kirby* was a tonic for any worker, whether in factory, field or office.

During all these years the good ship never met with any serious mishap, attesting to the carefulness of her skipper,

THE FLYER OF THE LAKES

Captain Arthur J. Fox, who sailed her for twenty-one of her years of island service. Captain Fox was the idol of all the island boys, each of whom vowed that someday he would be a master of a fine ship, stand upon the bridge and give orders to the men below. Many of those boys did follow the lakes for a livelihood and became masters of ships in due time.

The steamer *Frank E. Kirby* was named for a prominent marine architect and ship designer of Detroit who designed many of the large passenger and freight vessels of the Great Lakes and salt water. The *Frank E. Kirby* was of the paddle wheel type: 552. 91 gross tons, 203 feet overall length, and 55 feet beam over the guards, with nine foot draft. Her hull was of steel, and her engine was of the verticle beam type with the quaint walking beam above the top deck that rocked up and down while the vessel was under power.

This old familiar walking beam type of ship has disappeared entirely from the lakes. Even the sidewheel steamer is disappearing; there being only about a half dozen or so left, and these are all of the inclined engine type without the rocking walking beam. The old timers loved to watch the walking beam of a steamer as it would get under way. Close up, it was a huge iron casting usually taller than a man, and twenty-five feet or so in length, of double triangular design. At its tip ends were fastened the gigantic pistons coming from the engine itself. Always well oiled and smooth working, it would silently rock the hours away, day and night, good weather or bad, as the vessel sped along its course. The walking beam is a symbol of the bygone days of steamboating to the old timers.

197

MEMORIES OF THE LAKES

The *Frank E. Kirby* was built especially for this run at Wyandotte, Michigan, by The Detroit Dry Dock Company and came out new in June, 1890. She was owned by a group of Detroiters headed by Edward Dustin and Walter O. Ashley. Her engine, built by Fletcher and Harrison, had seen service in two other ships; first in the Revenue Cutter *John Sherman* and later in the passenger ship *Alaska*. Great care is given a ship's engines, and it is always a pride of the engineer to have the giant parts glide smoothly along with little wear. Such care, with occasional replacements, will cause an engine to run many, many years. The engine from the *Frank E. Kirby* is still in excellent condition. It is owned by Henry Ford's Edison Institute Museum and will likely find a permanent spot in this vast collection of engines assembled at Dearborn, Michigan.

The *Frank E. Kirby* maintained a daily schedule, making the round trip, between Detroit and Sandusky. She would leave Detroit at nine in the morning, head down river and into Lake Erie, calling at the islands of Put-In-Bay, Middle Bass and Kelleys Island. She arrived in Sandusky in time to coal and leave on the return trip at three in the afternoon. She made the same calls on the return trip to Detroit. Occasionally she would make a special run to Toledo or Port Huron. Hers was a well ordered and well regulated existence, and season after season found her serving satisfactorily all concerned.

The *Frank E Kirby* was famous as a fast ship. Her skipper often carried a broom at her masthead as a symbol of her speed. This was in the nautical code of the day when the broom indicated a clean sweep. She is reported to have had a speed of twenty-one miles per hour. A long pennant flew from the flagstaff atop her pilot house which proclaimed her the "Flyer of the Lakes." She put up a record of two hours and fifty-four minutes for the sixty mile run to Put-In-Bay from Detroit. This record has never been equaled and likely never will be, as in the old days the steamers could speed in the Detroit River while now they must check down owing to channel regulations.

In 1911 the owners of the *Frank E. Kirby* brought out the elegant new steamer, a propeller, *Put-In-Bay,* and the older ship was placed on a run opposite the new vessel. She continued on this basis until the close of the season of 1919 when she was withdrawn from service. During the following two years she lay idle at Detroit. By the opening of the season of 1922 she had been sold to other owners and was put on a run between Detroit and Kingsville, Ontario, making stops at Ecorse and Wyandotte, Michigan. In 1924 she was chartered to the Cleveland and Buffalo Transit Company to replace their burned steamer, *State of Ohio,* on the Toledo, Put-In-Bay and Cedar Point run. During 1925 she resumed her Detroit-Kingsville run.

During August 1926 she had her face lifted and her name changed. She became the *Silver Spray* and was placed on a cross lake run from Erie, Pennsylvania, to Port Dover, Ontario. However, as the *Silver Spray* she carried on only until May 1927, when her name was again changed, this time she became the *Dover.* Her route continued to be the same, Erie to Port Dover. Another side-wheeler, the *Erie* (formerly the *Pennsylvania* and *Owana*) was placed on the run opposite the *Dover*. The two ships gave daily service across Lake Erie until the close of the 1928 season when they were placed in winter quarters at Ecorse, Michigan. This marked the end of service for both vessels. While there they caught fire on the night of February 2, 1929. The *Erie* was a total loss while the *Dover* was only partially damaged. The following spring the *Dover* was rebuilt, but did not enter service due to poor business conditions. She lay thus until June 23, 1932, when fire again swept her. This time it spelled the end for the old flyer of the lakes as she was burned beyond repair. She sank at her slip and lay on the bottom until 1939 when she was raised and her engine removed. The balance of the wreck was disposed of as salvage scrap.

The *Frank E. Kirby—Silver Spray—Dover* had been a grand ship in her day. She had served a most useful purpose and brought satisfaction to all concerned. Like most of the latter day boats she did not end in a life-losing disaster. Instead, she contributed her remains to posterity by way of the smelters, so other steel might be forthcoming, possibly to be made into new, but not better, ships of the lakes.

Chapter Twenty-Two

THE WRECK OF THE WESTERN RESERVE

Whenever the old-timers of the lakes get together and chat of the bygone days, mention of the ill-fated freighter *Western Reserve* usually comes up for discussion. At the time of her sinking it was the talk of the lakes. A big ship for those days—three hundred feet long and forty-one feet beam with twenty-four feet draft—built of steel, and only two years old, the *Western Reserve* broke in two one night on Lake Superior and went down in deep water. To make it worse, her owner with his wife and two young children, and other invited guest passengers lost their lives in the tragedy. Only one man of the crew lived to tell the tale.

The *Western Reserve* was built for the Minch interests in Cleveland in 1890, and classified by Lloyds as A-1. Into the new ship went all the care and quality that shipbuilders then knew. She was the pride of the Great Lakes. Several times she hauled record cargoes.

On Sunday, August 28, 1892, her owner, Captain Peter G. Minch, himself an experienced lake skipper, with his wife, son, and daughter, aged ten and seven respectively, together with Mrs. Minch's sister and her little daughter, all boarded the *Western Reserve* at Cleveland for a vacation trip up the lakes. The freighter was without cargo and stood high in the water as she plowed outward past the Cleveland piers, bound for Two Harbors, Minnesota, for iron ore. In charge of the ship was Captain Albert Myers and Chief Engineer W. H. Seaman, both officers long in the Minch fleet.

The *Western Reserve* passed up through the Soo Locks without event on the following Tuesday at six in the afternoon. As the ship entered Lake Superior a moderate wind sprang up. The ship took shelter in Whitefish Bay, where the engines were stopped and the anchor run down. Since the wind did not increase, the captain and owner decided to continue into the open lake, and the ship sailed on.

The wind continued to blow and the waves mounted until they gave the *Western Reserve* a bad pounding. Still it was believed that the vessel could well stand such a sea. Suddenly a crack appeared on her deck, forward of the boiler house. With a wrench of the ship the crack widened, and the vessel broke in two. Passengers and crew all took to the two yawl boats.

In ten minutes the *Western Reserve* had gone beneath the rolling waves to the bottom of Lake Superior in six hundred feet of water. This happened about sixty miles northwest of Whitefish Point at nine in the evening of Tuesday, August thirtieth. The two yawl boats, after being launched with difficulty from the fast foundering steamer, were set adrift on the lake with the twenty-seven persons from the freighter. A short time later one of the yawl boats capsized in the heavy sea, spilling its occupants into the water. They were rescued by the other yawl boat. This dangerously overloaded the only remaining craft, as it headed shoreward with its cargo of shivering human freight.

When about a mile from shore, as it entered the broiling surf, the yawl capsized, dumping everyone into the white foaming water. Only one man was able to reach the shore. He was Harry W. Stewart of Algonac, Michigan, a sturdy wheelsman and an expert swimmer. Upon reaching the shore, at a point near Deer Park, Michigan, the lone survivor lay for awhile on the beach exhausted, and later trudged through the wild country to the life saving station twelve miles distant. There he told of his experiences and the loss of the *Western Reserve*. His one sad lament was that, had the yawl boat carried lights or flares, they might all have been saved, as they had seen the lights of an upbound freighter in the darkness of the night.

Last winter an old man died in Mentor, Ohio. He was Phillip J. Minch, son of Captain and Mrs. Peter G. Minch, who were lost along with his brother and sister, in the foundering of the *Western Reserve*. The comfortable home in which Mr. Minch passed his last days was named by him "Starboard Light". It was so called because that part of the ill-fated freighter was the only thing salvaged from the wreck. It floated ashore with some boards. The old gentleman had it wired, and it burned every night in his window as long as he lived.

The lantern has since passed to the Western Reserve Historical Society which has placed it on the front gable of the home of James A. Garfield, twentieth President of the United States, at Mentor, Ohio. Here at Lawnfield the starboard light remains as a silent reminder of the tragedy that befell one early steel freighter of the Great Lakes.

Note: Many marine men lay the cause of the foundering of the *Western Reserve* to the fact that the steel of which she was made was too brittle. When chilled by the waters of Lake Superior and pounded by the big waves, the strain was too great, causing the plates to crack. Long vessels are now made from steel that will withstand twisting and pounding without cracking.

‎⚓ ⚓ ⚓ ⚓ ⚓ ⚓ ⚓ ⚓

Chapter Twenty-Three
KAFRALU

The Great Lakes are studded with thousands upon thousands of interesting and picturesque islands. Life on these islands holds a charm all its own. It tends to make a person sufficient unto himself, and developes a certain ruggedness, even in this day. Many of the islands of the Great Lakes are carefully farmed; others are largely used by summer residents; still others are wild and uninhabited. Steamer service is available during the summer months, and on some of the more populated islands, daily airplane service is maintained throughout the year. In the winter many islanders go from one island to another, and sometimes to the mainland, in their automobiles by driving over the ice.

Any island formation is a peculiarity. Mostly consisting of rock or solid earth that has withstood the battering of years of storms with their consequent tearing down, these islands rise from the floor of the lake to above the surface of the water, and there offer man an unusual spot on which to live.

In the city of Sandusky at the turn of the century, lived a man who did much thinking about islands. He loved islands and the water that surrounded them. As he would bend over his bench turning leather into fine harnesses his thoughts invariably turned to sparkling wavelets rippling on an island's sandy beach; or to the campers on the shore enjoying the pleasures that an island affords. He wanted an island all his own! But a harness maker's income was small and the outlook none too promising, what with the coming of the automobile. It looked as if Louis E. Wagner would just have to be content with dreaming of an island, or with visiting one of the nearby Lake Erie islands on fine Sunday afternoons.

This might have satisfied a man of less determination than Mr. Wagner. He purchased a small boat and cruised about Sandusky Bay. His island dream persisted. One fine afternoon while in his boat cruising along the neck of land that extends far out into Lake Erie, known to millions of excursionists as Cedar Point, he noticed that the water level was exceptionally low. Presently his boat grounded on a sand bar. He sat there a long, long time, thinking and planning.

Here was a potential island! It required only more topping to be one. He was strong, and his sons were strong. Why couldn't they put on a topping and make a fine island out of this sand bar? Work? Sure! But constructive work was pleasure to Mr. Wagner. He could visualize something growing to be a source of pleasure to all. As he shoved his little boat off that bar, Louis Wagner determined to build his dream isle on that spot!

Returning home that evening he confided his plan to his wife, Kate. Seriously they talked it over, long after the supper dishes were put away. Kate Wagner knew her husband well. She believed that if he was determined to build an island, he would do that very thing. She would help him! Scoffers were aplenty as soon as the idea spread. It could not be done! If any sand bar was intended to be an island, nature would have made it one. Fall storms and winter ice would soon finish his island! A very foolish idea!

Carefully Mr. Wagner made his plans, and then set about to put them into practice. First, a scow was requisitioned. Before so very long he was hauling it regularly across Sandusky Bay, heavily loaded, and dumping everything imaginable on that sand bar; anything that would stay put. A nearby basket factory contributed a by-product known as "splints" and thousands of these went into the fill. Rocks, debris, earth, bricks, concrete, old iron, anything that the Wagners could gather together made up the fill.

Work? There was no end to it. Soon the tiny island began to appear above the shimmering waters of Sandusky Bay. More fill and still more! Hundreds of loads from the old scow went into the fill. Mr. Wagner was tired but happy those days. He was constructing something beautiful. Not beautiful as yet to the outsider—in fact very much the opposite, but Mr. Wagner had his plans.

Then came the cold winter day when a cabin was hauled bodily over the ice and placed atop the new island. That was definite progress. Now the island needed a name. Mr. Wagner had thought of this too. He wanted his wife and sons to be remembered and here was his chance. He would call his dream isle KAFRALU—KA for Kate, FRA for Frank, his older son, and LU for Louis, his younger son. Kafralu, that's what his island would be named! So it was, and so it is today.

Under Mr. Wagner's efforts the island continued to grow. Disappointments were many and heartbreaking. There was the time that he conceived the idea of pumping the silt from the bottom near the island, piling it high to be leveled later. He obtained the pumps and set to work. Two huge piles grew on Kafralu and Mr. Wagner went home humming. Then slowly but surely the piles disappeared. They just sank down into the greedy water and nothing of them remained. Then he saw that he needed piling or bulkheading driven around the island. So he proceeded to do this. An improvised pile driver was put to work. When next he pumped silt on his island it stayed there.

Came the day when a tree might be planted. So Mr. Wagner found a fine young willow and planted it. Then more willows. More cabins, too. Soon the island had seven cottages and some ninety trees. One willow now boasts of fifteen feet circumference. Summer cottagers flocked to Kafralu, and a dock was built to accommodate them. Boat service was maintained to the mainland.

Louis Wagner now had a new business. He was owner and operator of his own recreation island. To all outward appearances Kafralu was completed, but Mr. Wagner visioned still more. His hopes were cut short when he passed away in November 1941.

KAFRALU

Kafralu stands today as a monument to his dream and untiring energy. Many vacationists find happiness on its shores and health in its sunshine. They too share in a harness maker's dream of sparkling wavelets rippling on an islands sandy beach.

⚓ ⚓ ⚓ ⚓ ⚓ ⚓ ⚓ ⚓

CHAPTER TWENTY-FOUR

THE 1905 BLOW

It is late in the afternoon of Saturday, November 25th, 1905. The day is relatively calm for so late in the year and a dull sun is about to drop into Lake Erie.

A brand new bulk freighter stretches its five hundred twenty-five feet of length alongside the fitting-out dock at the American Ship Building Company's plant at Lorain, Ohio. The final activities are hurriedly being completed as the crew prepares for sailing. Everything is new and shining—shining as only a new ship can shine. Newness is everywhere; nothing save the wearing apparel of the busy crew is old. The galley is spotless with its well stocked larder, its stacks of substantial dishes and its attractive culinary equipment. The steward is the one man in the crew with new and clean white clothes. He is already busy with his helpers preparing the first supper to be served aboard ship. The big steamer is truly a fine accomplishment of the labors of man. Upon her bows and on her stern is painted the name *Joseph G. Butler, Jr.* The ship is about to join the busy fleet of Great Lakes bulk freighters engaged in the transportation of iron ore, coal, grain and stone, as well as lesser cargoes, to and from the ports along the shores which stretch from Minnesota and Wisconsin to New York and Pennsylvania.

210

THE 1905 BLOW

Leaving time! A last minute flurry as a party of five or six clean and prosperous looking men climb the ladder to the high deck. They are the owners and they are having an inspection and outing aboard the ship as she sails on this, her maiden trip. As is usually the case with the busy business man, time will not permit them to make the round trip, which requires about a week. They will leave the ship in the rivers and return to their offices by rail.

Adventure is in the air. Before the ladder is hauled aboard let us hurriedly climb to the deck in spirit and remain aboard unseen and take "come what may" aboard the new ship *Joseph G. Butler, Jr.*

In the pilot house and on the bridge men are taking their stations. Our captain, William P. Benham, is leaning out over his bridge rail, scanning carefully the length of the ship's deck on the dock side. The first mate is on deck supervising last minute details. Now we hear one of the most thrilling sounds ever invented. It comes from our deep-throated steam whistle. The tone is full, rich and very deep. The steam escaping from the instrument is an inspiring thing to see. Intensely white and with the apparent power of its mighty boilers, it blasts its roar over the waters and adjacent land for many miles. Farmers reading in the quiet of their homes in the early evening note that the freighters are running late into the season this year. The powerful steam dissolves itself with magic flourishes into thin air, once it has escaped from its tubes and valves of confinement. The echo rolls back at us. Another blast of the whistle and our ship starts to move slowly through the murky waters of the Black River.

MEMORIES OF THE LAKES

As is the custom when a new ship sails, all shore establishments and other ships in the harbor blow the departing ship a salute—three long blasts followed by two short ones—always answered by the new steamer. Never a more pleasant hail is to be heard than this distinctive salute between Great Lakes ships. Vessels in other parts of the world slide quietly past each other in the cold manner of strangers. Not so on the Lakes! Hail, brother, good luck and smooth sailing! A friendly greeting from one to another. A fine old custom among lake sailors. May it never end!

Darkness has settled now as our ship glides majestically through the old highway swing bridge, past the United States Life Saving Station, on down the river and into the lake. We are without cargo and therefore our ship rides high in the water. Soon the skipper will order the ballast tanks filled so that the vessel will ride deeper and consequently easier. Our destination is Duluth. We are to return with wheat for Buffalo.

The air is damp and chilly as we clear the Lorain Harbor lights. Only those of the crew whose duties demand their presence on deck are to be seen. The others seek the comfort of the cabins. The owners begin a tour of inspection of the interior of the ship in its every detail. Much time is spent with Chief Engineer "Bob" Smith in his spotless engine room, watching the huge shafts and levers move in perfect unison, all combining their efforts to move the giant ship through the water.

One can sense an air of extra precaution about the ship;

everything is new, brand new. Will it stand the test of stress and strain? The officers are carefully checking everything about the ship to make certain that all is well. Our course is set for the mouth of the Detroit River. Our speed is held down until the vessel has "found herself." Hour after hour the velvety black smoke rolls out of our huge stack to hang suspended in the air over the water, awaiting a faint breeze which will slowly expand its size and thin its bulk until, like the steam from the whistle, it too will dissolve into thin air. Our machinery continues to function perfectly. Over the fantail the wake of the ship can be seen foaming white in the darker water as our huge propeller churns our ship ahead through the night. All is relatively quiet now aboard the *Butler* with the exceptions of some occasional heavy laughter which comes from the cabin occupied by the owner-guests. Inspection over, they have turned to a game of cards to while away the time. The new ship *Joseph G. Butler, Jr.* is off to a good start.

The captain remarks to the mate, William Packer, regarding the unusually high barometer.

"Don't see it this high very often, Bill," he continues, "I'm not so strong for a too high glass or a too low one. A quick drop from where she stands now, to a low mark might bring us trouble. But, anyhow, right now everything's goin' along fine."

"Yes, sir, capt'n," replies the sturdy first mate, "but this late in the season the barometer is apt to behave funny. Well, we'll see."

MEMORIES OF THE LAKES

The mate is a dark complexioned, powerful man and has sailed the lakes for many years. His father also had sailed these waters. Eighteen years ago young Packer was the mate on the schooner *M. R. Warner*. While his ship was loading cargo at a dock in Ashtabula, a heavy gale sent Lake Erie on a wild rampage and drove all the ships on the lake to shelter.

It caught the three-masted schooner *James F. Joy* in its fury, and her skipper decided to come into the harbor at Ashtabula for refuge. But the storm was too much for the *Joy*, and distress signals were hurriedly hoisted. Word ran quickly among the harbor folk that the *Joy* was about to founder off the harbor.

"Who's a-goin' out to get her people off?" inquired Billy Packer aboard the *M. R. Warner*, when he learned of the plight of the *Joy*. Upon being told that there was no apparent intention of any help being sent to the foundering schooner, he called for volunteers to go out with him in his vessel's yawl boat. Quickly a crew was mustered. Ashtabula Harbor then witnessed one of its most heroic rescues. Billy Packer and his volunteer crew rowed their boat through the towering waves, while the wetness and chill of a late October storm beat upon them. After two hours of desperate struggling, they managed to get their boat alongside the sailing vessel, and Packer climbed to her deck.

He found the schooner a wreck; two masts had gone overboard; her remaining sails were torn to shreds; water was rising fast in her hold. He knew she could not stay afloat much longer. Nine men and a woman cook were aboard. The woman had been lashed to the remaining mast to keep her from being washed overboard. Packer cut her loose, and somehow managed to get the entire crew into his yawl, and they left the ill-fated *Joy*. As they looked back they saw the schooner go down by the head, lifting her stern into the air, and then plunging bow first to the bottom.

It took his friends fourteen years to get Billy Packer a gold medal for his bravery in bringing those ten human beings safely into Ashtabula Harbor. Eight years later he himself was shipwrecked when the schooner *Minnehaha* foundered in Lake Michigan. He was the sole survivor. Of such stuff are the lake men made, and this is the kind of men that made up the crew of the *Butler*.

Detroit is a sleeping city as we steam past at 4:20 Sunday morning. The fleeting glance up deserted Woodward Avenue as we go by its foot reveals but one "owl" street car. There are no pedestrians. We continue upbound past beautiful Belle Isle Park, now hooded in darkness, and then across little Lake St. Clair.

A dull day has just dawned when, as we reach the town of St. Clair, Michigan, on the St. Clair River, our owners clamber over the side into a waiting small boat and head for the shore. A bell jingles down in our engine room and our ship resumes her speed. Captain Benham waves from his bridge to the departing small boat and they return his salutation with shouts of, "Good luck, Bill."

It is just ten minutes past noon when we pass Port

Huron, Michigan, and Sarnia, Ontario, and a few minutes later we enter large Lake Huron. The lake is a dull slate-blue and the sky leaden. The wind is freshening; here and there the white crest of a wave breaks, indicating a restlessness of the water. The crew, now becoming acquainted with their vessel, settle into a regular routine. With the difficult navigating of the rivers behind him, our skipper goes below to look over his craft. The ship sails on.

Sunday turns into Monday as the big freighter plows her way up to the head of sullen Lake Huron. Fantastic lights of passing ships shape into a cold reality as they glide quietly by, only to return to another phantasm behind us.

Detour Reef Light is picked up on our port bow, and the skipper is called to take the bridge as we steam upbound through morning mist of the Saint Marys River. Our deep-throated whistle blasts the surrounding forests with our passing signals as we meet an occasional downbound steamer. Mud Lake and Hay Lake, just wide spots in the river, are passed, and now we blow for lockage up, at the great locks at Sault Ste. Marie.

Officials signal us to enter and we find our ship slowly steaming into a giant lock. In this same lock is the steamer *Bransford,* Captain "Doc" Balfour in command. The ponderous gates swing slowly shut behind us, and the two ships now begin a lift of some twenty feet, bringing us to the level of Lake Superior. The clear ice-cold water broils up from the bottom of the lock and the *Butler* is lifted bodily. In about fifteen minutes the broiling ceases and the gates at the head of the lock swing silently open. Our way is clear to proceed to the greatest body of fresh water in the world.

It is two-thirty in the afternoon of Monday , November 27th. The thermometer stands around twenty-eight degrees, and on the shore little puddles of water have turned into slick icy slides. With his greatcoat collar pulled up over his ears, our skipper leans over his bridge rail and moves his chadborne to signal our engineer to slow speed forward. Following in the wake of the *Bransford* we steam slowly out of the long lock into the grayness beyond.

"Feels like snow," the skipper remarks to the second mate as he enters the pilot house and removes his coat. "How's the glass?"

"Still very high, sir," replies that officer.

"It's too high for any good," observes the master.

The freighter ahead has pulled away and we increase our speed as Point Aux Pins Lighthouse is sighted on our starboard bow. Soon after, we pass Point Iroquois Light on our port side as we enter Whitefish Bay, the lower part of Lake Superior. The shore line fades into the distance as we steam out onto the big bay.

"I believe the glass has started to fall, cap'n," speaks the second mate as he scrutinizes the barometer.

"Let's hope it don't fall too fast," says the skipper. "Keep your eye on it."

217

MEMORIES OF THE LAKES

It not only fell fast, it plunged! Down, down, down, until the watching men wondered when it would touch bottom. In its fall it forecast what was to be the most disastrous storm that has befallen shipping on Lake Superior.

"It's snowing, sir," reports the lookout.

"And the breeze is freshenin'," remarks the mate.

"A fine kettle of fish," mutters the skipper. "Keep a sharp eye for Whitefish Light, bein' as how we're speakin' of fish."

"Yes, sir," answers the lookout.

Hard icy pellets clip against the pilot house windows and the rising wind whistles aloft. The empty ship is beginning to feel the action of the water.

"It's goin' to be hard to sight Whitefish if this snow gets much thicker," thinks the captain, but the words are not spoken aloud. No use borrowing trouble and then passing it out to the crew. They realize it nevertheless.

At dusk the faint flashes of the desired light are seen, and each man in the pilot house reports it simultaneously. A lull in the falling snow now helps to bring the flashes more vividly. It also brings to sight the lights of the *Bransford*.

"Looks as if Captain Balfour is taking her a bit to the north'ard," remarks our master, "but I'm goin' to keep a bit off to the south," he says slowly as though weighing his thoughts carefully.

218

THE 1905 BLOW

He instructs the wheelsman as to the course to steer as we come abreast of the light, and the big vessel turns slowly in the direction indicated.

A sudden gust of icy snow now envelopes the *Butler* and blots out all view, Whitefish Point Light, the *Bransford,* everything! We wonder when we will see that ship again. Her lights have been friendly, after a fashion, on this bleak evening. Now we are alone, unable to see even a ship's length ahead of us.

"Wind's freshenin' to the east, sir," reports the lookout.

"O. K.," answers the old man.

The wind loaded with snow by now is howling past our snug pilot house. The snow does not pile up on our decks, as the wind swirls it away and out over the water. Large combers are crashing against our bows and the ship is pitching and rolling heavily. Our whistle is blowing constantly—three short blasts, once a minute—the fog signal on the Great Lakes.

Our crew are not alarmed. To them such storms are to be expected at this time of the year on the lakes. They must hang on and see it through—just part of a sailor's life. Buffalo must have its wheat, come hell or high water. So keep her going and let's get the dirty weather behind us!

If the past day was bad, tonight is even worse. Hardly ever is it possible to see much beyond our steering pole. King Winter rules supreme. The thermometer is dropping nearly as fast as did the barometer. Huge waves are smash-

219

ing against the ship's sides, and she quivers from stem to stern.

"Good chance now to see what she's made of, cap'n," says the mate. "These rivets are sure straining. Let's hope those shipbuilders back in Lorain did a good job."

"She should be tight as a drum," replies the skipper, "but a good shaking up like this sometimes loosens a rivet or two."

"Ever hear about the *Western Reserve?*" asks the wheelsman, as he struggles with his wheel trying to keep the *Butler* on her course.

"Sure," says the mate, anxious to talk about something, even if it has to be a shipwreck—anything to break up one's thoughts. He continues, "Let's see, that wasn't so very long ago, 'bout thirteen years or so."

"It was on August 30, 1892," states the captain, who has an excellent memory when it has to do with shipping.

"And it was just hereabouts on Lake Superior that she foundered," adds the mate.

"Hell of a thought!" runs through the wheelsman's mind, but he says nothing.

The mate continues, "She cracked smack in two pieces. Couldn't stand old Lake Superior's pounding, tho' she was built of the best steel."

"Shipbuilders have learned a lot about strengthening these long vessels since those days. The unfortunate *Western Reserve* turned out to be what a guinea pig is to a doctor," explains the captain. "Folks learn by trial and error. Everyone thought that she was a fine ship when she left the shipyard, but she cracked in two, sure enough."

They all knew the story of how the freighter *Western Reserve* had sailed light from Cleveland, bound for Two Harbors, Minnesota. Her owner, his family and a party of guests were aboard. A gale blew up, and for a time the ship lay in shelter behind Whitefish Point, until her master thought it safe to venture out onto Lake Superior. She was a big vessel for her day, 2,392 tons burden. The seas proved too much for the *Western Reserve*. Her six passengers and twenty-five of her crew perished. A wheelsman was the only person to reach shore and live to tell of the strange fate that befell his ship.

No wonder there is a lull in the conversation now in the pilot house of the *Butler*. This story is not new to any of the men, but sailors are given to telling and re-telling their sea tales.

Our ballast tanks have long since been filled to settle the ship as low as possible in the water, but she is still much above the line at which she will ride when loaded with cargo. Everything about us is pitch dark, the sky, the air and the sea. It is impossible to picture this same spot as a beautiful scene in the summer with the sun shining on the sparkling blue water with a clear cut horizon in the distance. Winter in this north country brings a vast change.

During one of the infrequent lulls in the blizzard all hands scan the blackness anxiously for a familiar landfall.

MEMORIES OF THE LAKES

A series of distant flashes away to starboard! A short pause and they are repeated. It is the characteristic signal of Caribou Island Light! Probably for the ten billionth time, a mariner blesses the keeper of a light on shore. It is only a short glimpse, but long enough for the men in the pilot house. That is all they want. Now they can check their course for Keweenaw Point, where Gull Rock Light and Manitou Island Light should be our next welcome gleams.

A different motion now shakes the *Butler*—a series of quick vibrations.

"Throwing her wheel out," mutters the master.

Down in the engine room the chief engineer is making much more vehement remarks. Everything that is movable, and a few things that are not supposed to be, are sliding and slipping from one side of the room to the other.

As another succession of vibrations shakes the ship, the chief engineer springs to his levers. With all possible haste he shuts down the big engine to prevent it from racing, as the propeller comes out of the water. The giant seas are now tossing the *Butler* about so that at almost regular intervals our stern is thrown out of the water. This causes the propeller to whirl dangerously in free air, then hit the water again with a sickening thud which vibrates all over the vessel.

"Like one night on the old *Onoko*," the chief is telling his third, "I was a coal passer, and in a gale o'wind like this, one of our big iron wheelbarrows got loose and no one

222

would dare go to try and catch it. It would have broken every bone in his body if he had tried it. Well, sir, that old wheelbarrow would shoot from one side of the ship to the other on the smooth steel deck, like a high-powered automobile under full steam, and then crash itself against the steel side of the ship; then bang back again against the other side, and so on most of the night. They made good barrows those days, but this one couldn't take it. By morning it busted itself all up."

Now the chief is standing by his engine throttle patiently nursing her along—shutting her down when the stern rises out of the water, and opening her up when the stern is again in the water as it should be—so that the ship maintains her headway. Hour after hour through the long night this task must be done. Tedious, monotonous work, done in a hot steel-enclosed room while the walls and floor rise and fall precariously!

All the heroes of a ship are not on the bridge! Down below the deck of the engine room another group of men sweat and swear as they throw huge shovelfuls of coal into the roaring furnaces to maintain the steam pressure that drives the engines. They are the "black gang." Tough, sweaty and dirty, these men play a most important part in every coal-burning steamer. Many an unsung hero is down in the stokehold!

Hour after hour all hands stand by their various tasks. Hour after hour the northeaster continues to increase in velocity. Morning finds the big new *Butler* tossing and pitching like a cork in a mill race. Giant seas crash against the sides of the vessel and slosh across her decks. As the long hours continue, these huge combers increase in size as they beat full force across our decks in great walls of water ten to twelve feet high. This makes it impossible for the seamen to go from one end of the vessel to the other. They would be swept into the raging lake in an instant.

The telephone in the pilot house rings.

"Hello," bawls out the skipper into the transmitter.

"Capt'n this here is Weller, the steward. I just wanted to report to you that my two dining rooms are half full of water and it's sure raising hell back here."

"Where's it comin' from mostly, Weller?" asks the captain.

"Through the windows, capt'n," explains the steward, "I got a couple of waiters trying to let the water out through the door. They open it when the ship rolls high and close it when she comes down again, but it don't do much good. It's coming in so fast through the busted windows."

"Do the best you can, Weller, we're all having a tough time," counsels the master.

"O. K., capt'n, I just wanted you to know," and they both hung up.

"Steward's up to his waist in water back in the mess rooms," the skipper tells the mate.

"Won't need to take his bath on Saturday," remarks

the mate dryly, "but I'll bet the water's plenty chilly. Seems like there's no let up to this damned snow and wind."

Conversation is difficult in the pilot house as the wind shrieks around it. Our whistle is blowing "thick weather" signals, but much of its sound is lost in the storm's fury. There is nothing else to do but keep the ship headed as near to her course as possible. What headway is being made is very doubtful. The old man is doing his best to keep her going without unduly straining her.

"She seems to be taking it all right," he says to the mate, "there's plenty water in her hold, but Bob's pumped it there to help keep her wheel in the water."

"It's a day we won't forget in a hurry, cap'n, eh?" says Packer.

"It sure is," answers Captain Benham.

All day long the men aboard the *Butler* stand doggedly at their posts and all that night. What rest they get is under the most trying circumstances.

"We got to keep her well off Keweenaw Point, Bill," says the skipper.

"But how are we going to know where Keweenaw is, with all this damn blizzard about us?" asks Packer.

"We won't," replies Benham, "but we'll have to keep her well off anyhow, see or no see."

And keep her off they did! Unable to see a thing on that raging water and being continually shaken violently by the giant seas that oftimes send the spray flying over her smokestack, her crew stick wearily to their jobs, each man doing his utmost. The men in the forward part of the ship have not been able to get aft to eat, but meals are all but forgotten by each individual as he stands by his duty. Two husky mates attempt to open a pilot house door. With all their strength they push together. The door strains and opens but not over two inches. The gale blasts into our quarters. They close the door and abandon their efforts.

While Lake Superior is a very large body of water, the mariner must always watch that his ship is kept away from its rocky shores. Unlike his salt water brother sailor, who can ride out a storm for days knowing that there is no land within hundreds of miles and no consequent fear of crashing his ship on the land, the lake sailor must always be wary of piling his vessel up on an exposed shore.

This often means it is necessary to turn the craft around and head in another direction until the storm has subsided. Turning a ship in a high sea is no little task. Too often she is caught in the trough of a giant wave and, unable to climb the precipitous sides of the waves, she is sometimes washed upon the shore, be it smooth sand or rocky cliffs.

So it is now with the ice-coated *Butler,* just before dawn breaks on this eventful Wednesday on raging Lake Superior. Captain and mate discuss their situation at length and decide that they should turn their vessel around to keep her in deep water. With a master stroke of navigating and considerable good luck, the *Butler* is turned in that heaving sea and heads back into what the officers hope is open water.

"Snow's easin' up, cap'n," reports mate Packer. "It can't keep it up forever."

"Might let up at daybreak," observes the skipper.

By six o'clock the storm has abated and the snow has ceased to fall. Captain Benham wraps himself up in his sweaters and greatcoat and ventures out of the pilot house to climb the slippery icy mast aloft, to make an observation. Steam hangs over the water as over a giant boiling kettle.

"Air is so much colder than the water, likely brings it about," says the captain to himself as he scans the open waters above the steam for a familiar landfall. It is bitter cold, some ten or so below zero. His eye catches a gleam above the morning mists. He notes the flashes. He waits until it is repeated and then he carefully climbs down the mast and enters the pilot house.

"Outer Island Light," he announces triumphantly, and gives orders to set a new course that will put the ship right for Duluth.

"Guess it's about blown itself out now, cap'n," says Packer, referring to the storm.

"Seems so. Wind's easin' too. Guess we'll get along all right now," replies Captain Benham.

"I was a might bothered about the Apostles," says Packer. "Those Islands are bad for a ship in our position just before the snow stopped. I wonder if any of the boys piled up on one of them this time."

"Only good luck would keep them off," Benham replies, then continues, "My brother, Charles, is out here somewhere with the steamer *Wm. S. Mack*. Hope he is all right. He's due in Duluth 'bout same time as we were, 'afore the storm struck. Maybe he's in ahead of us, we'll see."

"Charles'll come through all right," assures Packer. "That *Wm. S. Mack* is a good ship. We'll all be on the lookout for him."

Heavy seas continued to roll the *Butler,* but the fury of the storm is past, and the lake continues to rise in long swells in sullen remembrance. Our crew now begin to get some well earned rest. Captain Benham takes a short nap, his first sleep in about fifty hours. He has not had his clothes off since we left Lorain. Crew member relieves crew member as the *Butler* steams along toward Duluth.

Off the port of Two Harbors, Minnesota, almost thirty miles from our destination, our lookout lowers his binoculars and calls out, "Steamer *Bransford* off our starboard bow."

Sure enough, there just ahead of us is the *Bransford!* We recall the last we saw of her was away back off Whitefish Point, just at the start of the storm.

"We'll have to make it a point to talk with Captain Balfour when we get to Duluth and see how they came along," remarks Captain Benham, "but I'm mighty glad to see him now. He must have had a bad time of it too."

THE 1905 BLOW

"Another steamer some distance ahead of the *Bransford*, sir," reports the lookout, "headin' for Duluth."

After a time we make her out as the *Perry G. Walker*, and we subsequently learn that she had sailed from Duluth two days previously. She had suffered heavy damage and was now returning to Duluth to await developments. It was her captain who reported later that the small lighthouse on the end of the Duluth pierhead had been washed off and was floating on the lake.

At last the city of Duluth is sighted. This city, rising abruptly from the water's edge, is built on the side of a high hill, resembling somewhat the rim of a deep saucer. It stretches for some twelve or fifteen miles along this hill and almost every building has a view of Lake Superior from some of its windows.

The harbor is the St. Louis Bay and is formed by a long thin arm of solid land extending out into the lake. This land is called Minnesota Point. Parallel stone piers have been constructed at the mouth of the harbor to form a deep channel to the lake. Between these two long piers must pass all the shipping that enters and leaves the twin ports of Duluth, Minnesota, and Superior, Wisconsin. These cities are rated as the second largest shipping ports in point of tonnage in the United States, being exceeded only by New York City.

All hands aboard the *Butler* are intensely alert as we near the harbor. Here we shall learn what the storm did to other ships caught in its fury. Binoculars scan the still swelling waters. We sight the barge *James Nasmyth* at

229

anchor some distance from the harbor, loaded heavily with iron ore and coated from stem to stern with ice. Later we were to learn she had been spared from disaster by sheer good navigating mixed with good luck.

"There's a ship broadside to the ship channel, to the north'ard of the pier entrance, Bill," says our skipper as he hands Packer the glasses, "and she looks pretty bad off."

"Great Caesar! She certainly is bad off!" ejaculates the mate.

Captain Benham's face is grim. Could that be his brother's ship the *Wm. S. Mack?*

"Can you make her out?" he asks quietly.

"Hard to tell from here, but seems like she's a 'steel truster'. Yes, sir, I can make out her stack now, tho' it's all coated with ice. That's a 'steel truster' sure 'nuff," replies Packer as he hands the glasses back to his skipper.

"That's what she is!" exclaims our master.

He heaves a long sigh. At least it is not Charles' ship, as she belongs to another fleet.

"Too bad, too bad! Some chaps have had plenty trouble in her," the captain continues as he scans the unfortunate vessel. "She's coated with yellow ice all over."

"Yellow ice?" queries the mate. "Must've been in shallow water where the bottom was picked up by the sea and then thrown over her. I don't like yellow ice. I'll take mine clear if I have to have ice," he concludes.

THE 1905 BLOW

As we approach the harbor it is clear to see that the storm has wreaked havoc with shipping. The vessel sighted proves to be the bulk freighter *Mataafa*. She lies helpless on the bottom in shallow water with a large crack in her sides amidships.

"Broken in two or three pieces," mutters our skipper. "She's sure a wreck! And a mighty good steel ship too, the *Mataafa* was."

On the other side of our vessel, lying inside the harbor hard aground is the big freighter *R. W. England*, blown there in the seventy-five mile an hour gale that swept Duluth Harbor the day before.

The clock in our pilot house shows it to be noon as we steam into the harbor and head for our elevator dock. Up on the streets of the city can be seen great drifts of snow.

"Higher than a street car," remarks mate Packer, as he looks at the huge masses of snow ashore. "They've sure had some storm, sure enough!"

The *Butler* is warped into her berth. Her first one way trip is over. Her ladder is freed of snow and ice and lowered over her side to the dock. A uniformed messenger boy calls up, "Telegram for Captain Benham."

As the skipper reads it he grins and hands it to Packer.

"It means you too, Bill," he says.

Packer reads it aloud, "Congratulations on a fine bit of steamboating."

It was signed by a prominent vessel owner of the lakes.

231

"I'd keep that, cap'n, as a sort of trophy," says Packer, "and it will always remind you of one of the worst storms we ever saw."

The skipper folds it and tucks it into his inside pocket.

"I'm agoin' to keep it, Bill, and for just that."

The weary skipper drags himself off to his room for a well earned rest. He removes the clothes he had donned just before sailing from Lorain. His was the responsibility of bringing a new ship, worth close to a half million dollars, and its crew of some thirty men, safely into port.

The afternoon is spent in rest by all of the crew not essential in port. To most of them it is the first real rest that they have had since the ship left Sault Ste. Marie. Examination of the *Butler* for damage by the storm finds much in a small way—the covering on pipes running under the deck has been washed away by the constant sloshing around of the eight feet of water in the hold. This water has also washed off all the paint on the underside of the hatches. In the dining rooms and galley considerable damage resulted. Many windows and ports have to be replaced, but nothing of any great consequence in the structure of the ship has been damaged.

That evening, outfitted in his warmest garments, Captain Benham leaves his ship to visit at that famous eating and gathering place for lake captains, Lanigan's. Here the real tales of the storm are told by the men themselves, not boastfully—for many of them are not proud of what has happened—but actual accounts of their experiences, be it good fortune or bad. Sitting at a large round table

232

in the center of the eating house are five or six men. Captain Benham is warmly received as he joins the party.

Newspapers litter the table and show signs of much use by the men. These papers tell the stories of many of the mariners that are not in Lanigan's this evening. Many ships are still overdue. Some of them mentioned are: *W. E. Corey, R. L. Fryer, H. B. Nye, Umbria, E. F. Holmes, Victory* and her barge *Constitution, John Stanton, Wm. S. Mack, Phillip Minch, Angeline, W. D. Rees* and the *Spokane.*

The ships that arrived during that day are reported as: *George J. Gould, Henry W. Oliver, George Stephenson, Maricopa, F. M. Osborne, George H. Russell, R. E. Schuck, Thomas Maytham, Neptune, Wm. A. Reiss, Uranus, Bransford, James B. Eads, Barge 117, Yosemite* and *Joseph G. Butler, Jr.*

The weather man reported that the wind blew between seventy and eighty miles per hour, and that the storm raged two days and two nights. The temperatures varied from zero to twelve below. Special editions and out-of-town papers are brought in by the host and placed upon the tables. One such special reports the safe arrival of the freighter *Wm. S. Mack* and others in Duluth. Another lists the boats lost and stranded as follows: *Ira H. Owen,* foundered on Lake Superior; *Western Star,* stranded on Lake Superior; *Vega,* wrecked on South Fox Island, Lake Michigan; *Lafayette,* wrecked near Encampment Island, Lake Superior; her barge *Manila,* ashore at same place; *William Edenborn,* wrecked on Split Rock, Lake Superior;

her barge *Maderia,* ashore on Split Rock; *Mataafa,* wrecked at Duluth; *Crescent City,* ashore near Duluth; *Isaac L. Ellwood,* disabled in Duluth; *W. E. Corey,* stranded on Michigan Island; *Coralia,* ashore near Point Isabelle; Barge *Maia,* ashore at same point; *George Spencer* and schooner *Amboy,* wrecked off Thomasville; *Monkshaven,* wrecked near Thunder Cape, Lake Superior.

Many overdue ships are being reported hourly as arriving in port or in shelter with more or less damage. The freighter *Umbria* is reported safe in Duluth Harbor after a hazardous experience. Caught in the gale enroute to Duluth, her pilot house was torn open and much of it went overboard. Her compass went with the wreckage. Her captain and wheelsman were forced to use the after emergency steering wheel. With the storm raging about them, as this wheel is unprotected from the weather, and without compass to guide them, they worked their vessel along the north shore of the lake and brought her safely into port, heavily coated with ice and snow. Here, in the safety of the harbor, her captain stepped on deck and fell, painfully fracturing his forearm.

The *Isaac L. Ellwood* made the harbor of Duluth and then sank from the damage sustained during the blow. The *Bransford* punctured her bottom by striking on Isle Royale, but was able to continue on her way and made port.

The group of captains at the table scan the columns of the newspapers with great interest to learn the fate of the still missing ships.

234

THE 1905 BLOW

The wooden schooner *George Herbert* foundered in the blow off Two Islands on the north shore of Lake Superior. Her crew of five are believed to have perished with their ship.

The freighter *W. D. Rees* arrived in Duluth safely, but had a badly twisted rudder, which made steering exceedingly difficult.

The freighter *C. Tower, Jr.,* is safe in Lily Pond near Houghton, Michigan, where she limped to shelter. Bound from the upper lakes to a Lake Erie port with iron ore, she was caught by the full fury of the storm. Her crew stated that it would have been impossible for the vessel to have gone farther, as she would certainly have foundered. Her starboard bulworks were crashed open and her steam pipes were broken. She had three feet of water in her hold.

Safe arrival is mentioned of the steamer *Angeline* at Sault Ste. Marie after a hard trip down Lake Superior with a cargo of ore. The storm struck her off Keweenaw Point, and it was a battle to reach the safety of Whitefish Point. Her captain was on duty for forty-eight hours without rest.

The wooden steamer *Cartagena* with the wooden barge *Grampian* in tow was long overdue at Sault Ste. Marie and, for a while, grave fears for her safety were felt. The two vessels arrived safely at the locks, but were badly iced and showed signs of a severe battering.

The freighter *Victory* and her barge *Constitution,* bound for a Lake Erie port, were loaded with ore and were about off Keweenaw Point when the storm struck hardest. The tow line parted and the barge was lost astern of the steamer. Unable to locate her in the blizzard the *Victory* proceeded, and after a terrific struggle reached Sault Ste. Marie and reported the missing barge. The *Constitution* drifted at large about Lake Superior, a victim of the storm. All shipping was notified to be on the lookout for her in the event that she had survived the storm. At last the steamer *C. W. Moore* sighted the helpless barge off Copper Harbor, Michigan, her steering gear gone. She got a line aboard and towed the barge to safety. Lady Luck had ridden the *Constitution* most surely and had kept the big barge from being washed ashore on some rocky island or barren beach.

Outside in the wintry night huge bonfires are built and kept roaring in the darkness on the Duluth waterfront to aid ships that are still out on the lake trying to make port. Many a skipper later extended his thanks for those timely beacons as he came safely into the harbor.

The group of mariners in Lanigan's increases. The latest newspaper states, "The storm is the most disastrous in the history of lake shipping, fifteen steel vessels were wrecked, but only one of that class foundered. That was the *Ira H. Owen* which carried with her nineteen lives. All the other steel boats were driven ashore."

The last seen of the *Ira H. Owen* was when she was sighted by the steamer *Harold B. Nye* some forty miles off Outer Island at the height of the storm on Tuesday. The *Owen* was sounding distress signals and appeared to be in a bad way. However, the *Nye* herself was having great difficulties and was unable to go to her assistance. Snow then set in and fell for two hours. When it cleared the *Owen* was not to be seen. Her wreckage was found later by the steamer *Sir William Siemens*. About the time that the *Nye* sighted the *Owen* the mate of the former vessel was washed overboard and lost.

The wreck of the 430 foot, 6,900 ton, steel freighter *Mataafa* is probably the most spectacular of any on the Great Lakes. Her tale is told around the table in the smoke filled room of the eating house.

The *Mataafa* was loaded with a cargo of iron ore and had in tow the steel barge *James Nasmyth* of 5,800 tons capacity and 366 feet keel length, also loaded with ore. The vessels were bound for a Lake Erie port. Daylight of Monday, November 27th, was waning as the *Mataafa* and her consort cleared the long stone piers of Duluth Harbor out onto the open lake. Little did their crews think that they were sailing right into the gathering storm. *Mataafa's* skipper had sixteen years of Great Lakes sailing experience behind him and a staunch ship only six years of age with which to cope with the weather. Ordinarily he would have won. But shortly after clearing the harbor he found the seas were breaking over his decks from both sides. A blizzard had set in which cut his visibility to but a few yards. They smashed onward, however, through the wild night until four the next morning. Then her skipper decided to return to Duluth, as it appeared likely that both vessels might founder if he were to continue on his course. They managed to put about and head back to Duluth.

For a while they anchored in the open lake and rode out part of the storm. Then it was decided to run on into the harbor.

It was afternoon before the *Mataafa* arrived off the Duluth piers. The storm was still raging furiously, and it was decided to drop the *Nasmyth* a safe distance out in the lake at anchor, as it would have been impossible to navigate the steamer and the barge through the narrow harbor entrance. The *Nasmyth* dropped her hook and there rode out the storm in safety.

The *Mataafa* continued on and was almost abreast of the pierheads when she was caught in a current which swung her to the northward. Her bow veered toward the north pierhead when a big wave raised it and, as it came down, it crashed on the shallow bottom. This upset her navigation, and in a moment she had crashed her bow against the stone pierhead with a sickening thud that badly dented and punctured her prow.

For an instant it looked as if she might still make the harbor, as after she hit she veered off slightly and her bow ran a little inside the piers. Would the wind and current carry her through? It was not to be. The long ship began to swing broadside to the entrance. In such a position the *Mataafa* would soon be wrecked. The captain decided to go back to the open lake. Further ill fortune followed the vessel that afternoon. Just at this most critical moment something went wrong with her machinery, and the big ship was left to the mercy of the elements.

All this happened as hundreds of people stood in the

stinging cold of the storm on the Duluth waterfront and witnessed the losing battle of the *Mataafa*. The situation of the vessel was such that no help could be sent to her. After her power failed she was caught by wind and current and was driven clear around to the north pier where she went aground. But the storm was not yet through with the *Mataafa*. Tremendous waves now beat upon the vessel and pounded her until she began to break apart. Pictures taken of the ship in this situation show giant waves crashing over her with the spray flying higher than the tips of her masts.

About half the crew were in the stern which was slowly sinking to the bottom. Three of them made their way perilously along the deck to the shelter of the forward cabins. Nine men perished in the after end, due to exposure. The fires under her boilers had been extinguished, as the stern settled, leaving the men without heat. Reports tell of finding the bodies of the men encased in ice in the after end. Some had sought shelter in the ventilator hoods and had to be chopped free. One engineer was encased in ice behind the stack.

The men in the forward part spent a horrible night huddled together in the captain's cabin. The water shot through its broken windows and covered the floor. They had to move and jump about constantly to keep up their circulation.

The life saving crew managed to shoot a line to the ship but it was useless as it froze before a breeches buoy could be rigged. There was no food, and for water the men broke off icicles and sucked them.

Rescue came with morning. The life saving crew contrived to get a boat to the wreck and the half frozen men were taken ashore and given treatment.

Not far from the ill-fated *Mataafa* another of her fleet was having tough going. This was the steamer *Crescent City*. Two miles east of Lester Park in Duluth she was blown ashore. No lives were lost. Her crew put a ladder ashore and left the ship much the same as they would have done at a dock.

The freighter *Lafayette* with the barge *Manila* in tow came to grief on the rocky north shore of Lake Superior, eight miles from Two Harbors, Minnesota. The *Lafayette* was blown on the rocks at the height of the storm and her tow, the *Manila,* crashed into her. The *Lafayette* broke completely in two, but her crew were able to scramble to shore.

The *William Edenborn* was dashed onto Split Rock on the north shore of Lake Superior. Her consort, the barge *Maderia,* broke in two and one man in her crew was lost.

The Canadian steamer *Monkshaven* crashed on Angus Rock, north of Isle Royale in Lake Superior, and sank. Her crew were rescued.

The flagship of the Pittsburgh Steamship fleet, the *William E. Corey*, struck hard upon Gull Island Reef, Michigan Island, Lake Superior.

The steamer *Western Star* went aground near Fourteen Mile Point, Ontongon, Lake Superior, with little damage and was released and reached her destination, Duluth, in a few days.

240

THE 1905 BLOW

The wooden steamer *George Spencer* and her consort, the schooner-barge *Amboy*, ran ashore at Thomasville, sixty miles east of Two Harbors, but their crews were rescued. They were bound up the lakes, light, for ore cargoes.

The freighter *Coralia* with the barge *Maia* in tow went hard aground on Point Isabelle, Lake Superior.

All the storm damage, we learn, is not confined exclusively to Lake Superior, though it did strike heaviest there. Lake Michigan took a hand in wrecking the steamer *Vega* of the Gilchrist fleet, on South Fox Island. This freighter had left Ashland, Wisconsin, with a load of iron ore for South Chicago during a snowstorm the evening of November 25th, and had locked down at the Soo on the 27th. Her difficulties occurred after she reached northern Lake Michigan. Indian fishermen helped rescue the crew.

Seven miles north of Chicago, at Glencoe, during a snowstorm, a ship's whistle signal of distress was heard. It was later learned that it was the freighter *German*. She became lost in the blizzard while bringing down a cargo of iron ore from Lake Superior to Chicago and went ashore at Glencoe. Her crew were rescued.

The passenger steamer *Argo* of the Graham and Morton Line, bound from Chicago to Holland, Michigan, missed the harbor entrance at Holland and went hard aground. A hero emerged from the shipwreck in the person of a member of the life saving crew. After they got a line aboard the *Argo* it became apparent that those on the stricken steamer were unable to rig up the breeches buoy in a satisfactory manner, thus preventing the passengers and

241

crew from being brought to shore and safety. Sensing the difficulty, one daring member of the life saving crew tied a line fast about his body and sent the other end of the line to the stricken vessel. He was then dragged through the icy waters between the shore and the ship. Arriving safely aboard he proceeded to rig up the breeches buoy. Soon it was carrying the passengers and crew to safety.

The freighter *D. C. Whitney* stranded in the storm near Port Washington, Wisconsin, on the west shore of Lake Michigan.

Lake Huron too had its wrecks, though most of the ships on this lake were able to find shelter from the storm. The wooden schooner-barge *Olga* broke away from her towing steamer during the storm and was unable to find the steamer. After drifting about in a sinking condition her crew took to the yawl boat, and were later rescued by the passing steamer *Winslow*. Unmanned, the barge continued to drift about the lake, becoming a severe menace to shipping. She went ashore on the beach three miles north of Goderich, Ontario, a total loss.

The wooden steamer *Charles M. Warner* went on at Nine Mile Point, Cheboygan, Michigan, but was released. The steamer *L. C. Smith* was also reported stranded near Nine Mile Point.

Another wooden schooner-barge the *H. Bissell* broke loose from her towing steamer and went to pieces off Alpena, Michigan.

While steaming up the St. Clair River in the storm, the

wooden freighter *Saginaw* went ashore three miles below Port Huron, caught fire and burned to the water's edge. Her crew were saved.

The little wooden steamer *Point Abino* stranded in Lake St. Clair and broke up in the gale.

The big wooden freighter *City of Rome* went ashore on Middle Island in Lake Erie during the storm, but was released and towed into Cleveland Harbor.

There were many other minor strandings both of wooden vessels and steel ones, but these mentioned are the major ones and attracted the most attention of the lake men clustered around the tables in Lanigan's, those anxious days and nights of the 1905 blow.

NOTE: There are sailors living today who went through the 1905 blow who will tell you that it is the worst ever to occur on the Great Lakes. They may be right. There was but one other, the "Big Storm of 1913" that can compare with it. True, more ships and lives were lost in the latter storm than in the one told here. Measured by that yardstick it exceeds the 1905 blow. Nevertheless, the old-timers will tell you that the 1905 blow had more snow, wind and seas than anything yet seen on the Great Lakes.

This 1905 blow was two score years ago, and many of the ships mentioned in this tale are still active in lake service. It should be borne in mind that the navigating of those days is not to be compared with present day navigating. Every disaster brings its improvements. Fore and aft life lines were made compulsory after this storm. The newest vessels have inside passageways, making it unnecessary to go outside on deck. Wireless was unknown then on lake ships. Today the radio telephone affords instant communication between ships and shore. Direction finders enable the lake mariner, beset with blinding snow or fog, to find his exact location regardless of the visibilty. Improved weather forecasts from government stations and between the ships themselves are a great aid. The gyro compass has earned its place aboard ship.

The wooden steamer has disappeared entirely from the lakes. Rescue ships and planes are constantly maintained completely equipped for immediate action. They are manned by United States Coast Guard trained personnel. Construction too, has improved greatly. What happened to vessels in 1905 has been carefully studied by ship building engineers and the defects have been remedied. Vast strides have been made toward safe navigation and shipping since the blow of 1905.

The ship *Joseph G. Butler, Jr.* is still active on the Great Lakes. She is now the *Donald B. Gillies*. The *Mataafa, Wm. Edenborn* and *W. E. Corey* are at present in service. The *Crescent City* and *Coralia* are reported inactive. The barges *Manila* and *Maia* are still in commission. The engine of the *Lafayette* was salvaged.

⚓ ⚓ ⚓ ⚓ ⚓ ⚓ ⚓ ⚓

CHAPTER TWENTY-FIVE

THE KALIYUGA

The little group in the tug office were earnestly discussing the conditions under which the many vessels of the Great Lakes had "sailed away" never to be heard from again. Such ships as the *Chicora, Bannockburn, Alpena, Marquette & Bessemer No. 2, Cerisoler, Inkerman, Rouse Simmons, C. F. Curtis, Annie M. Peterson, Seldon E. Marvin, Clifton,* tug *Cornell, Kamloops, Milwaukee, D. M. Clemson, Anna C. Minch, William B. Davock* and others were mentioned.

"Ever hear of the *Kaliyuga?*" queried Old Timer.

"*Kalee* who?" responded one of the group.

"The stout wooden steamer *Kaliyuga*," answered Old Timer. "She was lost on Lake Huron in 1905 and never a trace of her was found. She was a darned good ship, too. And with a good skipper, engineer and crew. Nobody ever found out what happened to her. She just sailed away," he mused.

"Let's hear about her," the group chorused, and they settled back to listen. Old Timer's stuff was always good!

"Well, let's see, it was about a month afore the big 1905 storm, and that was late in November. That would make it in October. Guess nobody ever really knew exactly when

245

the *Kaliyuga* did go down. Musta been around the 20th or so, I reckon. She had loaded iron ore at Marquette, on Lake Superior, and was bound down to some Lake Erie port to unload. The weather was bad that fall. Heavy early snowstorms and high winds. Lots of the older schooners and steambarges were wrecked that season. Well, the *Kaliyuga,* she was in the Cleveland Cliffs fleet, passed down the Soo all right real early one morning and that was the last she ever had a line on shore. The skipper of the *Frontenac* told later of seeing her about four that afternoon some seven miles off Presque Isle Light in Lake Huron. The master of the *L. C. Waldo* also reported seeing her about dark between Middle Island and Thunder Bay Island headed east. A gale o'wind was blowin' and it got worse and worse and kicked up a terrific big sea. That was the last ever seen of the *Kaliyuga.*

"Cap'n Fred L. Tonkin of Painesville, Ohio, sailed her, and her chief engineer was from Cleveland, Charles A. Sharpe. It was Cap'n Tonkin's first ship, although he had been her skipper for two seasons afore.

"Well, all hands waited for the *Kaliyuga* to report in at Port Huron, but she didn't. We had no fang-dangled radio telephones or such in those days. Nobody worried much, however, as she was one of the strongest and best wooden steamers on the lakes, and well kept, too. Some five years afore this the *Kaliyuga* was long overdue and she showed up all right. She had been caught in a gale o'wind and had lost her rudder. So no one was unduly alarmed when she didn't show up just exactly on schedule. They believed she would come along. They figgered that maybe she put

246

in for shelter som'ers along the east or north shores of Lake
Huron, mebbe even around Manitoulin Island. Her sister
ships of the Cliffs fleet searched hard for her, as did all
the boats, but nothing was ever reported.

"Each day things got more tense as nothin' was heard
or seen of the *Kaliyuga*. Her owners sent out tugs after
the wind let up to scour the lake for signs of her, but to no
good. They all came back with nothin' to say. No wreckage, no nothin'. She had sixteen men and one woman
aboard. Well, that's all there is to tell. She didn't ever
show up and nobody ever knew where she went down, nor
why. I recollect that she was eighteen years old when she
was lost. Had been built at St. Clair, Michigan, and it
seems to me that she would be about 270 feet long and
40 feet beam, and likely drew about 21 feet. She was quite
a boat, was the *Kaliyuga*.

"Oh, yes," he added, "her owners had quite a shock at
the height of the search for the ship, yes, sir, quite some
shock. Into their office walked the second mate of the
Kaliyuga, well and strong as could be. It seems he missed
his boat when she sailed and his name was still listed as
in her crew. Just a lucky guy. Fate does those things
sometimes."

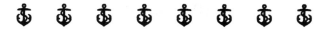

Thousands of ships freighting millions of tons of cargo pass annually through the Saint Marys Falls Canals. These waterways have become known by the shorter name of Soo Locks. Both the United States and Canada maintain locks for shipping. There is no charge to the vessels of any nation for lockage in the canals of either country. Canadian shipping uses the American Locks as freely as do the ships of the United States. The same is true of the United States vessels using the Canadian Lock.

On the United States side there are four locks abreast while on the Canadian there is but one. A single lock in each of the canals lifts the boats, or lowers them, between Lakes Huron and Superior. The lift is twenty-two feet under normal conditions. Time required for lockage averages about twenty minutes. It is an impressive sight indeed to watch a huge freighter containing some twelve thousand or more tons of iron ore being gently lowered from the level of Lake Superior to that of Lake Huron. The giant ships are all handled by their own power—no tugs or shore towing machines are used, as in some of the world's large canals. The long ships steam into and out of the locks as gently and quietly as though moved by a magic hand. Accidents are almost unheard of in locking through.

248

THE SOO LOCK ACCIDENT

One big accident—the one which is still talked about by the old timers—occured on June 9, 1909, in the Canadian Lock. Business was brisk at the canal that day and the lockmasters were hustling to get the ships through and on their various ways.

The lock was filled to the Lake Superior level, on this particular occasion, and the palatial Canadian Pacific passenger steamer *Assiniboia* was made fast in the lock about to be lowered to the Lake Huron level, twenty-two feet below. The Pittsburgh Steamship freighter *Crescent City* was behind the *Assiniboia* waiting to enter the same lock so that the two vessels could be locked down together. The *Crescent City* was slowly entering the open gates at the upper end of the lock.

Under usual conditions these upper gates would be closed behind the freighter as soon as it had entered the lock and was made fast. Then the excess water would be let out of the lock and the two ships lowered to the Lake Huron level. Then the lower gates would swing ponderously open and the ships would steam out of the lock and on their way down the lakes. But fate decreed differently this day.

Below the locks, expecting to lock up after the *Assiniboia* and *Crescent City* had left the lock, slowly steamed the bulk freighter *Perry G. Walker* of the Gilchrist fleet. Her captain was on the bridge, and it was evidently his intention to tie up to the Canadian shore a safe distance below the lock to permit the downbound ships to pass. He signaled to his engineer to stop and then to reverse, preparatory to making a landing. To his utmost astonishment his big ship sprang to full speed ahead. He frantically rang for reverse but still the vessel continued to plunge forward. The channel narrowed to the lower gates of the lock and toward it swept the *Perry G. Walker*. Before anything could be done to prevent it, the bow of the ship struck the lower gates tearing them from their fastenings.

Bedlam prevailed instantly in the canal. With the upper gate still open, a wall of twenty or more feet of water with all the weight of Lake Superior behind it, came crashing out of the now open lock. The *Assiniboia* was torn loose from her moorings by the onrush of water beneath her and shot down the stream completely out of control. She hit the *Perry G. Walker* a glancing blow and her anchor tore a hole in the side of the freighter above the water line. Her captain wisely ordered full speed ahead on his engines so that he might obtain some steerage way to help guide his racing ship.

The *Assiniboia* tore on into the more open reaches of the river below and finally came to comparatively calm waters. She was little damaged by her unique experience. Her cargo had shifted slightly, it was reported, and a few plates in her sides were loosened, but otherwise she was none the worse for her fast ride.

The *Perry G. Walker*, completely out of control, was whirled around several times by the maelstrom, and finally grounded on a shoal out of the channel. She too, oddly enough, received little actual damage.

THE SOO LOCK ACCIDENT

The *Crescent City,* heavily laden with ore, was a different story. She was engulfed in the swirling waters and swept down stream like a feather. In her mad rush through the lock she tore a great hole in her side as she swept past the broken lower gate. Then she rushed on, overtaking the *Assiniboia,* and striking her two glancing blows, as she swept on down stream.

Tug crews on the United States side of the Saint Marys River below the locks watched with astonishment as this swift action raced before their eyes. Always alert to any emergency, the tug men hurriedly cast off their lines and sped after the *Crescent City.* She was overtaken as she reached more quiet water. They took her in tow back to the American Soo, and reached there just as the big freighter settled to the bottom in shallow water.

Fortunately no lives were lost in the accident. Estimated damage to the locks ran around a quarter of a million dollars, and to the *Crescent City* around one hundred thousand. A few days later the *Perry G. Walker* steamed on her way, as had the *Assiniboia.* Soon after, the *Crescent City* was temporarily patched and raised and brought to Cleveland. She is listed as arriving in that port with ore on June 12th. Captain Frank Rice of the *Crescent City* later remarked to his skipper friends that he was certain he had made the fastest locking record for steamboats ever hung up, and none of them challenged his statement.

Stopping the rush of water and bringing the lock into service proved to be a real task. Engineers worked night and day in an effort to bring the rushing water under

251

control. A movable dam, designed for use in such an emergency, did much to help. Leaf by leaf it was slowly and with great difficulty placed into and against the racing waters, and gradually the flow was checked. Many other efforts were also made simultaneously and they proved effective, but the Canadian Canal was out of commission for some time after its rough treatment by the big ships.

♀ ⚓ ⚓ ⚓ ⚓ ⚓ ⚓ ⚓

THE "WELLAND CANALERS" OF WORLD WAR I

The First World War found the United States with practically no merchant marine upon the high seas. Foreign competition had long since forced it out of business. Much was talked about it, but little was really done. We had some coastal ships and a few on the Great Lakes that could be sent promptly to salt water, but those were all the vessels that could be mustered.

The cry went out from Washington for ships, ships, and more ships. It echoed around the Great Lakes. Ship builders began to figure. Immediately it was discovered that the bottleneck from the lakes to the sea was the Welland Canal. Its locks limited the size of the ships that could be built for foreign trade in the many fine ship yards on the Great Lakes. But a small ship was better than no ship at all. And thus it was that the so called "Welland Canalers" came into being—so named because they could just squeeze through that bottleneck between Lake Erie and Lake Ontario on their way to the seven seas.

Other canals through which the vessels also had to pass before reaching tidewater are the Galops, Rapide Plat, Farran's Point, Cornwall, Soulanges and Lachine Canals. All these canals are owned and controlled by the Canadian Government. They are built around rapids and shoal

253

waters in the St. Lawrence River. While small for ocean traffic they were larger than the Welland Canal Locks of those days. All served to help drop sea bound ships down to the level of the ocean.

Since that time the Welland Canal has been rebuilt and can now handle any ship afloat on the lakes. The St. Lawrence canals are now the bottleneck. However, a ship of reasonable size can now make her way from salt water into the Great Lakes without difficulty. In the years prior to the Second World War a regular freight service was maintained by one or two foreign steamship lines, each with a fair sized fleet of ships, from ports on the Great Lakes directly to ports of Europe. This service is now being resumed. Let us return to the Welland Canalers of the First World War.

The details in the construction of the Welland Canalers varied some, but in the main they were pretty much alike. The lake shipyards with their husky riveters and skilled workers went to work with a will, and soon the trim little ocean vessels were sliding sideways down their ways in considerable numbers. Most of them bore a name beginning with "Lake" on their bows. For instance there were the *Lake Arline, Lake Gormania, Lake Farge, Lake Fernando, Lake Medford, Lake Pachuta, Lake Agomak, Lake Chelan* and *Lake Narka*. There were others that did not bear such names, like the *Craycroft*, and the *Crawl Keys*. There were the "collier" type too—all lake-built that went to the sea. There was also the larger type of freighter that was cut in two after completion and thus hauled through the canals to tidewater, there to be put together again.

254

THE "WELLAND CANALERS" OF WORLD WAR I

The builders were proud of all these ships. Into each of them went honest toil along with the thought that one day each of these vessels would be called upon to do her utmost in battle, be it with the sea or with the submarine of the enemy. They wanted their ships to stand every test. The men who build a ship have as much right to be proud of her as do the men who sail her.

Even winter did not slow up the work of constructing these ships, though it did impede their delivery. It was necessary to await the ice thaws in the spring before the winter-built vessels could be sent seaward. Many exciting races with fast forming ice were held by the crews in the late fall and early winter, trying to get their ships through the lakes and into salt water before the ice held them fast.

The somewhat abrupt ending of the First World War in November, 1918, ended the construction of the Welland Canalers. Most of them were delivered to tidewater, and many saw foreign service. Many others never made a trip across the sea. After the war they were laid up in out-of-the-way places to accumulate rust and rot. They could not be operated on the high seas in competition with foreign-owned ships and still earn a profit for their owners. The American merchant seaman is the best paid sailor on the seas, and lives the best aboard ship. Commercially the Welland Canaler was decidedly out of the running in any foreign trade.

However, many were used in the coastal trade and many returned to the Great Lakes. The well known Poker Fleet hauling package freight on the lakes was comprised mostly of these Welland Canalers. They were renamed *Ace, King, Queen ,Jack* and so forth. Others, like the renamed *Aetna, Frank J. Peterson, J. J. O'Hagen* and *Saginaw* went into private owners' hands, and served on the Great Lakes until the start of the Second World War.

However, as stated, a great number of the Welland Canalers were never used, and after lying at anchor for many long months, they were sold by the government for scrap. The Ford Motor Company dismantled many of them for this purpose at its Detroit factories, and the trim ships found their way into the blast furnaces. The Ford organization, however, did alter some of them into barges and operated them in their business on the Great Lakes. They carried the "LAKE" names: *Lake Allen, Lake Crystal, Lake Farge, Lake Folcroft, Lake Freeland, Lake Frugality, Lake Frumet, Lake Hemlock, Lake Inaha, Lake Kyttle, Lake Louise, Lake Pleasant* and *Lake Sapor.*

The United States needed ocean ships equally as badly at the start of hostilities in the Second World War as it had in the First World War. All the available Welland Canalers were at once taken over by the government and hurried into sea service, once again to serve their country in time of dire need.

The minimum dimensions of the locks of the Welland Canal at the beginning of the First World War were: 270 feet length, 45 feet width and depth of 14 feet. The maximum size of vessels which could be accommodated with safety was: 261 feet overall length, 43 feet 6 inches beam and depth of 13 feet. After reaching tidewater these ships could load again as much cargo as was on board through the canals, the depth of the ships being up to 28 feet 2½ inches for overseas shipment.

Several records were made in the construction of the Welland Canalers—one for time of building, stood until beaten by another method of construction during the Second World War by a Pacific Coast yard. The Great Lakes record was made on the *Crawl Keys* at the Great Lakes Engineering Works at Ecorse, Michigan. Thirty-four calendar days elapsed between the keel laying and the delivery of the 3,500 ton deadweight steel freighter. At that time this was a world record. The keel was laid on July 11, 1918, and the ship was launched 16 calender days (14 working days) later. On August 13th the *Crawl Keys* was completed, and on the following day was accepted and placed in commission.

Statistics showed that 508 rivet gangs working in the lake yards averaged 2,290 rivets per gang, per week, exceeding by 30 per cent any other shipbuilding district. Also with one-tenth of the total United States shipbuilding space, the lake yards built one-fifth of the total tonnage delivered. The lake shipbuilders are very proud of these records and of the subsequent performance of their ships. They have estimated that, if all the vessels they built during the First World War were placed prow to stern, they would reach for a distance of nine miles—truly an imposing exhibition of what the builders on the lakes contributed to the winning of World War I.

MEMORIES OF THE LAKES

The old Welland Canalers served well in the Second World War—served with the Merchant Marine, the Navy and the Coast Guard all over the world. The Great Lakes yards build good ships.

⚓ ⚓ ⚓ ⚓ ⚓ ⚓ ⚓ ⚓

CHAPTER TWENTY-EIGHT

SAILOR COUPLE

She called him "Peg." I never learned why. She was a bright-eyed, keen little woman of about three score and ten, and he was her husband, a worn old man, whose days were numbered. I had called, along with his physician and another old friend, for a chat with him about his bygone sailing days. I should say THEIR bygone sailing days, as since their marriage, she had been his constant companion, afloat as well as ashore.

We were in their tidy little house on the outskirts of Sandusky, Ohio. A home-made sign on the porch read "SNUG HARBOR".

In a faltering voice he told of his experiences as skipper of Great Lakes windjammers. Occasionally he hesitated, trying to recall a definite incident accurately, or the name of a particular boat. Carefully following his every word, she never failed to supply the required detail.

Their story started a little over fifty years ago, when he was the young and husky captain of the sturdy wooden sailing schooner *Massasoit* hailing from Milwaukee. One day the charming lady of this story signed two important articles. The first was a certificate of marriage to him, and the second, as cook aboard the *Massasoit*. Thus the

259

schooner was their honeymoon ship, and in it they set sail upon the long voyage of life.

Maritally, the sailing was smooth enough, but the actual sailing had all the storms and strife that come the way of those who choose to live before the mast. Many tilts with death together had welded their lives into an inseparable lifelong companionship. The sea can do that.

I ventured a remark intended to be a bit humorous, to the effect that she was doubly bound to execute his orders, as her captain as well as her husband.

"But she never did!" he ejaculated.

Turning to her he suggested that she tell of their experience on Lake Erie during the "Big Storm of 1913."

"He likes to tell that one about me," she said, and added, to him, "You tell it yourself, Peg."

And so Captain Charles L. Goodsite told of that wild November night aboard the heavily laden wooden schooner-barge *Our Son* of which he was then master and she the cook. They were bound down the lakes in tow of the lumber steamer *C. H. Green* with the schooner-barge *Genoa* also in the tow. The trio had left the shelter of the Detroit River. As night fell, they headed across storm-tossed Lake Erie toward Buffalo, two hundred and forty watery miles to the east.

All the old-timers recall that terrible night on the Great Lakes when upwards of two hundred and fifty sailor folks lost their lives, and eleven lake ships slipped beneath the waves. There was no wireless communication on the ships in those days. A man afloat knew only of his own plight and could only surmise the fate of his brother mariner also caught in the storm.

"About midnight it got real bad," the skipper recalled. "The snow was so thick we couldn't see the lights of our steamer. The wind whistled and began to lift big heavy planks from our lumber cargo on deck and whirl them away into the night. We rolled and pitched somethin' terrible.

"I thought about Minnie below in our cabin, and decided it would be handy if she got dressed, and maybe put on a life jacket. Couldn't tell what might happen. So I went down and told her to get her clothes on and stand ready."

"And I did just as he told me," she interrupted.

"Well , yes, she did, but then again, she didn't. She got dressed all right and got her life jacket on, but she didn't like sitting there with all those duds on, and so she takes them all off again and gets back in bed, and when I came down later just to see her, there she was, sound asleep," he chuckled.

"I wasn't worried. I knew he would bring us through all right," she declared, "and he did."

The Goodsites were not the only couple to sail the lakes as captain and cook. It was fairly common practice in the old windjammers. Sometimes whole families shipped in the schooners. Even today aboard the big freighters, man and wife often serve as steward and assistant.

Captain Goodsite stuck mostly to the sailing vessels, even after these had passed into oblivion. With their tall masts cut to stubs, and the vessels themselves converted into schooner-barges, to be towed behind a more steady steamer, the Goodsites continued to sail in them. They loved those ships. Captain Goodsite did command an occasional steamer, but his heart was in the windjammers.

"Was the work hard?" I asked.

"Oh, like any job, it had its hard work," thoughtfully answered the mariner, "But then, too, it had its easy moments. I mind the season we had the *Annie Laura*. She was outfitted for salvaging, and we went to work on the old *Pewabic*, which was sunk in 1865 in almost two hundred feet of water about twelve miles out of Alpena.

"That was sure a soft job. All I had to do was to pilot the *Annie Laura* out to the wreck in the morning and anchor her there while the wreckers went to work, and then take her back again in the late afternoon. And some days when the weather was too bad, we didn't go out, but we got our pay just the same. Yes, sir, that was a soft job, at least for those days."

The captain continued to reminisce.

"We did right well for the owners on that job, too," he said quietly. "Brought up tons and tons of copper that brought big money during the first World War. The

Pewabic had a big cargo of the stuff when she sank. Lots of other things came up too, ship's furniture and dishes, folks' belongin's, and even skulls and other bones. Yes, sir, that was a soft job."

The grand old sailorman began to show signs of fatigue. His physician suggested that we leave. Minnie asked us to wait a moment and she disappeared. In an instant she returned with a good-sized picture in a well worn frame. It was a penciled drawing of the *Massasoit*, in full detail.

"Billy Young, one of our crew made it for us," she explained, "and every rope, sail, and spar is correct. Please take it. I know you will appreciate it."

That old drawing of the *Massasoit* is one of the author's choicest possessions and hangs in a favored spot on his office wall. It is reproduced for the readers of this book in the pictorial section.

Some sixty days later Captain Charles L. Goodsite passed away at Snug Harbor.

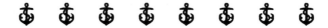

Chapter Twenty-Nine
THE 1940 ARMISTICE DAY STORM

Clyde Cross, husky commercial fisherman, owner and skipper of the gasoline fishing tug *Three Brothers*, remarked to his wife on the eve of Armistice Day, 1940, that it was a good thing that their house was well built, for were it not, the storm that was raging outside might blow the place down. Clyde dropped another log on the fire. His living room was cozy.

The modest Cross dwelling stood not far from the beach in the quaint little town of Pentwater, Michigan, which lies about midway up the eastern shore of Lake Michigan.

The wind shrieked and swirled stinging particles of hard snow and ice against the window panes. It also carried grains of white sand from the nearby high dunes which line the shore at this point. The thermometer flirted with zero.

"Bad night for the men on the lake," Cross continued.

"Just listen to those waves roaring against the shore! Pretty early for such a stiff blow."

It continued to blow violently all that night. Clyde Cross was not the only man who feared for the safety of seamen aboard ships on the open lake that wild night. Residents along the entire west coast of Michigan watched the gale and heard the raging waters.

THE 1940 ARMISTICE DAY STORM

Early the next morning Gustave Fisher, friend and fellow fisherman, came to the Cross door. The wind was still blowing and carried with it more snow. He stamped and brushed it off as he entered.

"Mornin', Clyde," he called. "Darn bad night, eh! I hear that there's a freighter ashore up at Juniper Beach."

"I'm not much surprised," replied Clyde. "That wind would have blown any ship way off her course. Let's try going down and see her."

Their car struggled along the storm-drifted country road that stretches the eight or ten miles southward along the shore. During a let-up in the swirling snow they made out the hull, deck houses and masts of a medium-sized freighter. Giant waves were crashing over the vessel, and she was thickly coated with ice. No smoke came from her stack, nor were there any other signs of life aboard the stricken ship. She lay hard aground, parallel to the shore, with her bow headed northward, about a third of a mile out.

The two fishermen stopped their car and looked silently at the shipwreck.

"S'pose there's any one aboard her, Gus?" asked Cross of his companion.

"It sure don't look like it," he replied. "If there is they must all be frozen."

They returned to Pentwater, each man silent with his own thoughts.

265

MEMORIES OF THE LAKES

All that Monday Clyde Cross watched the lake and thought of that wrecked ship covered with ice, being pounded to pieces by the waves. Were there any people aboard? The gale slowly diminished in velocity, and with it the waves quieted some.

That night Clyde Cross drove back to Juniper Beach for another look at the shipwreck. He could barely make it out in the snow dimmed darkness. Look! What was that he saw? Were his eyes playing a trick on him, or was it his imagination? No, it was real! A steady dim light glowed mournfully from the forward part of the ship! There must be some life aboard that ice covered wreck to make that light. Cross watched that tiny glimmer a long time and then, chilled through, he went back home.

He slept fitfully. That ice covered ship with the one feeble gleam of light kept him restless. He began to figure how he could get out there and see for himself what was wrong.

By morning the lake was somewhat calmer, though the snow continued to fall. Cross had made up his mind to take his twenty-two year old tug *Three Brothers* and go out there to the wreck. Gustave Fisher and Joe Fountain volunteered to go along as crew. They had no heat aboard the tug, but they managed to get her clattering old Buick engine started. By nine o'clock the antiquated forty footer was churning her way through the sullen icy waters of the Pentwater River, headed for rampant Lake Michigan.

Meanwhile the newspapers of the country had learned of the effects of the storm. In glaring headlines they told of the wrecking of many ships on the Great Lakes, of the heavy toll of lives, and of the heroic struggle of many other ships that, though badly battered, were able to limp into port.

The *Three Brothers* with its shivering crew of three headed for the wrecked steamer. They had learned that she was the Canadian freighter *Novadoc*, two hundred fifty-three feet long, built in 1928. She was enroute from South Chicago to Fort William, Ontario, with a cargo of powdered coke. The courageous little fishing tug chugged her way through the tossing waters and eventually pulled alongside the stranded steamer.

Ten nearly frozen men were huddled in the forward cabin. With great difficulty they were transferred to the bobbing little rescue boat. They told of seven others that were in the after end of the wreck. Two of their number had already perished by being washed overboard in attempting to crawl from the after end to the forward end. Cross and his crew then maneuvered the *Three Brothers* to the stern of the wreck and there took aboard all seven of the trapped seamen.

The seventeen men rescued included the captain and the chief engineer. All were in grave danger from exposure and hunger. Several had frozen feet. For thirty-six hours, ever since the ship had gone ashore, they had crowded together in the small forward cabin, or the galley aft. An ordinary oil lantern was their only source of heat and light. The *Three Brothers* chugged her way safely back into Pentwater harbor where Clyde Cross landed his grateful passengers.

MEMORIES OF THE LAKES

Word of the daring rescue was quickly spread by the newspapers, and soon Clyde Cross and his crew found themselves heroes. Telegrams and letters poured in to them from the folks of two countries, congratulating them on their efforts. Clyde Cross values one of those letters in particular. It is from an elderly couple in Canada, and it thanks him and his crew for saving their sailor son—painstakingly written, and worded as only a devout and thankful mother and father could write to the courageous men who had saved their boy's life at the risk of their own.

Only a few know how close Clyde Cross, his crew, and the survivors all came to going down in their overcrowded fishing tug in the icy waters of Lake Michigan on their return trip to Pentwater. Subsequent examination found that a good-sized hole had been stove in her starboard bow about one inch above the waterline, and her skeg and stem had been badly twisted on her strenuous rescue mission. Repairs were duly made and the *Three Brothers* resumed her fishing duties. Clyde Cross was awarded a medal by the Canadian Government as a token of appreciation for his part in the heroic rescue.

The *Novadoc* still lies stranded where she came ashore that eventful night. Eventually she broke in two amidships. Several unsuccessful attempts at salvaging the vessel have been made, but the wreck still defies all efforts.

The ill-fated *Novadoc* was not alone in her struggle that same wild night on Lake Michigan. Within what normally would have been the range of her whistle, two other staunch bulk freighters were fighting a losing battle to keep afloat. They were the *William B. Davock* and the *Anna C. Minch*. Both of these ships were lost with all on board.

Nothing has ever been gleaned from either vessel as to the exact cause of their founderings. The *William B. Davock* is reported to have carried radio equipment, but no communication was reported received from the ill-fated boat. Lake Michigan swallowed them both and left but few crumbs.

The four hundred and twenty foot *William B. Davock* was not an untried ship. For thirty-three years she had plowed the waters of the Great Lakes. Probably her most thrilling previous adventure was during a severe storm in December, 1909, on Lake Erie. For several days the ship was unreported and feared lost, along with the carferry *Marquette & Bessemer No. 2*, which succumbed to the waves with all hands in the same vicinity. The battered *William B. Davock* finally made port.

On her fatal trip, begun on Thursday, November 7, 1940, the *William B. Davock* left Erie, loaded with coal for South Chicago. She carried a crew of thirty-two men in charge of Captain Charles W. Allen of Detroit. Usual November sailing weather prevailed, and the freighter maintained her average running time. At noon on Sunday two steamers were reported passing up through the Straits of Mackinac, one was the *Dalwarnic* and the other was the *William B. Davock*. That was the last definite reporting of the latter ship.

269

Four hours later that same Sunday, the three-hundred and eighty foot Canadian freighter, *Anna C. Minch,* in command of Captain Donald Kennedy, also passed up through the same Straits. She too made her last report at that time. What happened after the two ships entered broad Lake Michigan can only be surmised.

Certain it was that the center of the storm swirled about the two ships and they were tossed about violently. Falling snow undoubtedly obscured their vision. Shrieking winds must have made their whistle signals futile. Probably even their pilot houses and cabins were demolished in the maelstrom, and the vessels may have become unmanageable. Seams may have opened.

As the storm abated vessel owners awaited word from their ships. One by one they were accounted for, all but the *William B. Davock* and the *Anna C. Minch.*

Three days after the storm had blown itself out, Clyde Cross while cruising about looking for wreckage, located a spar protruding from the water, a mile and a half south of the Pentwater pier. Further investigation convinced him that he had located the wreck of the *Anna C. Minch.* It lay in forty feet of water, some four hundred feet off shore. He rushed the news to shore. Divers hurried to investigate and, upon going down to the wreck, learned for certain that Clyde Cross was correct—it was the *Anna C. Minch.* Rather, it was one-half of that ship—just the forward half, minus the pilot house and forward cabins. A gaping hole, twenty feet in length on her port side near the bow, with the plates curved inward, was reported by the divers. Vessel men think that this hole might have been cut there by the prow of the *William B. Davock* during the height of the storm. The after part of the *Anna C. Minch* was never located. Her Collingwood, Ontario, skipper and his unfortunate crew of twenty-four Canadian seamen perished in this wreck.

The exact location of the wreck of the *William B. Davock* has never been definitely ascertained, but it is thought to be not far from that of the *Anna C. Minch,* inasmuch as wreckage and bodies from both ships washed ashore together.

The 1940 Armistice Day storm raged over the entire lakes area, but seemed much more violent on Lake Michigan, particularly in the region of Pentwater and Ludington on the east shore. Wind velocities were reported from a generally prevalent eighty miles an hour to one hundred and twenty-six miles an hour at the lighthouse on Lansing Shoals in northern Lake Michigan.

Still farther to the north the two hundred and fifty-three foot ocean-type freighter, *Frank J. Peterson,* without cargo, was hurled on a shoal at St. Helena Island not far from the Straits of Mackinac. Her crew were later rescued and the vessel, after being abandoned the following winter, was salvaged and returned to service.

To the westward of the *Frank J. Peterson,* the four hundred and sixteen foot gravel carrier *Sinaloa* was in difficulty, and ended by being blown ashore some three hundred feet off Sac Bay, at the tip of the Garden Peninsula. Here again good fortune, in the form of United

States Coast Guardsmen, rescued the crew. The ship was abandoned for the winter, but was salvaged the following summer.

Near Manistique, Michigan, the four hundred and fifteen foot self-unloader bulk carrier *Conneaut* was reported to have lost her propeller and rudder as the mountainous waves beat her. She was washed ashore. Two days later she was pulled back into deep water.

At the south end of the lake, off South Haven, Michigan, two husky fishing tugs were lost—the *Indian*, a forty-eight footer with a crew of five, and the *Richard H.*, a steam tug with a crew of three.

Up on big Lake Superior the three hundred and eighty-five foot freighter *Sparta* was hard ashore on a rocky ledge of the Pictured Rocks, some fourteen miles east of Munising, Michigan. Her difficulties had occured a few days earlier than the Armistice Day storm, November fifth, to be exact. Bound for Duluth without cargo, the *Sparta* left the Soo in clear weather. Some twelve hours later she encountered strong northwest winds that shortly developed into a gale estimated by the crew to be about sixty-five miles per hour. One difficulty after another beset the *Sparta*, with the result that she drove up between Grand Portal and Miner's Castle, two of the picturesque high rocks that are viewed by hundreds of sightseers every year. The captain and five men made their way in a sail-rigged life boat to Munising through tremendous seas, and there reported their plight to the Coast Guard Station.

THE 1940 ARMISTICE DAY STORM

The crew were all safely removed, but the *Sparta* spent a lonely winter on that desolate shore. Spring brought the salvage crews who eventually removed the wreck, and towed it to a shipyard for repairs. She later was returned to service.

The foregoing were the heaviest losses of the 1940 Armistice Day storm, but many other craft and their crews had harrowing experiences before arriving safely in port.

Among these was the three hundred and ninety foot carferry *City of Flint 32*. This sturdy ship was caught off the harbor of Ludington in the seventy-five mile an hour wind. Missing the breakwater, she went aground in the height of the storm. Her seacocks were opened and she was allowed to settle on the bottom to keep her from pounding. By means of an eight hundred foot breeches buoy, rigged in the biting cold by the Coast Guardsmen, the few passengers were brought ashore. The crew stayed aboard, and after the storm the vessel was pumped out. With the aid of a tug she was soon floating in deep water.

The package freighter *Alfred H. Smith,* two days overdue, made port at Milwaukee on Thursday, November fourteenth, her deck loaded with battered automobiles, some leaning crazily over her sides, and her hold a shambles of wrecked refrigerators, cases of sardines, chocolate, and other freight. Two cars went overboard from the ice coated and wind swept deck.

The tanker *New Haven Socony* was long overdue at her East Chicago destination. Fears that she was lost were rising when she limped into that port, heavily coated with ice, with her superstructure badly pounded by giant seas. Her pilot house roof had been torn away, and was reported found on the beach near Grand Haven, Michigan. So heavily weighted down with ice was the tanker that her decks were within eighteen inches of the surface of the water.

Other vessels reported safe but damaged were the *Justin C. Allen, Crudoil, Arthur Orr, Empire State, Mercury, Irene,* and many others. When the lakes subsided, vessel men counted some seventy lives lost, two freighters and two tugs lost, five vessels ashore, and millions of dollars worth of damage to shipping in general.

Twenty-seven years before, to the very day, in 1913, raged the "Big Storm" of the Great Lakes. This great storm is usually considered by lake men to have been the worst ever experienced by shipping on the Inland Seas. Eleven freighters were lost and two hundred and thirty-five persons perished. Oddly, this Big Storm did not strike Lake Michigan in its greatest fury. In fact no craft of any consequence was lost on this lake, while the 1940 Armistice Day Storm struck principally upon Lake Michigan and almost avoided the other Great Lakes.

As is usually the case after all great disasters, investigations reveal where new safeguards and improvements can be made. So it was with the 1940 Armistice Day Storm. Vessel owners promptly ordered new safety equipment installed on their ships. Great sums of money are spent each year for the safety of men and ships. Today, life aboard Great Lakes vessels is probably safer than being abroad on the streets of a great city, or on a teeming cross-country highway.

⚓ ⚓ ⚓ ⚓ ⚓ ⚓ ⚓ ⚓

ACKNOWLEDGMENTS

During the six years that I have been assembling the material for this book I have been greatly helped by many folks—far too many to be mentioned here by name. I am particularly indebted to Captain William P. Benham, dean of lake skippers, for his kindly interest and valuable assistance in many of the details. I am appreciative of the interest shown by the following lake steamer masters: Captain Frank E. Hamilton, Captain Severn Nelssen, Captain Richard W. England, Captain Charles F. Meyers, Captain Varn L. Hosner, Captain John C. Mier, Captain John C. Murray, Captain Fred L. Ermish, Captain Ambrose Knudson, Captain H. J. Scheible, and the late Captains Charles L. Goodsite and John V. Trowell.

Many of the lake shipping offices have contributed accurate and detailed lore. Outstanding in this respect is Mr. Oliver S. Dustin of Detroit. The officers and men of the United States Lake Survey Office of the War Department, Corps of Engineers, at Detroit, were most helpful and courteous.

So many steamboat enthusiasts have aided in the gathering of some of the material that I am sure to omit some names through sheer oversight. I recall many pleasant hours spent with the following well informed gentlemen: William A. McDonald of Detroit, Louis Baus of Cleveland,

ACKNOWLEDGMENTS

Wilbert G. Schwer and Dr. William F. Burger, both of Sandusky, Jewell Dean of Cleveland, Clyde Cross of Pentwater, Robert G. Morrison of Cleveland, Clarence S. Metcalf of Cleveland, and Eugene Herman of Cleveland.

By correspondence much help was received. Such men as Carlos C. Hanks of Providence, Chief J. G. Dickinson of the U. S. Navy, Herbert R. Spencer and William L. Morrison of Erie, Lewis G. Castle of Duluth, Rev. F. C. St. Clair of Manitowoc, Fred Landon of London, Joseph Bayliss of St. Joseph Island, and many others, have contributed greatly.

Libraries also proved most helpful and courteous. I am particularly appreciative of the work done by Donna L. Root of the Cleveland Public Library and the late Elbert Jay Benton who made available the valuable collections of records and papers of the Western Reserve Historical Society of Cleveland. The public libraries at Milan, Ohio, and Sandusky, Ohio, Sault Ste. Marie, Michigan, and Duluth, Minnesota, were also very helpful and attentive.

Last but by no means least, I want to acknowledge and thank the many kind readers of my previous book, LORE OF THE LAKES, who took the trouble to write to me some of the finest and most inspiring, interesting, and informative letters that I have ever read.

THE AUTHOR

⚓　⚓　⚓　⚓　⚓　⚓　⚓　⚓

BIBLIOGRAPHY

So great a number of references have been consulted during the preparation of this book that I confess I am at a loss to recall each and every one. It may have been but a date from one reference, or a name from another, and the title of the publication has since slipped my mind. There were many old magazines, leaflets, booklets, newspapers, passage lists, directories, and the like, to which I refer in this remark.

There are several excellent current books relative to the ⁞Great Lakes that are most worth while. Particularly of interest was Walter Havighurst's THE LONG SHIPS PASSING. Articles by Mr. C. H. J. Snider that have appeared for many years in the Toronto Telegram under the title SCHOONER DAYS are marine gems.

In my personal library are many books, magazines and papers to which I have often referred in the preparation of this work. The list follows:

Bayliss, Joseph and Estelle: HISTORIC ST. JOSEPH ISLAND. Cedar Rapids, Iowa, 1938.

Beasley, Norman: FREIGHTERS OF FORTUNE. New York, 1930.

Beers, J. H., & Co., HISTORY OF THE GREAT LAKES. Two volumes. Chicago, 1899.

BIBLIOGRAPHY

Beeson's Marine Directories: Chicago, 1887 and later years.

Bulletin No. 54, U. S. Lake Survey. Detroit, 1945.

Channing, Edward and Lansing, Marion Florence: THE STORY OF THE GREAT LAKES. New York, 1912.

Cleveland News: Daily newspaper. Cleveland, Ohio.

Cleveland Plain Dealer: Daily newspaper. Cleveland, Ohio.

Cleveland Press: Daily newspaper. Cleveland, Ohio.

Clowes, Ernest S.: SHIPWAYS TO THE SEA. Baltimore, 1929.

Curwood, James Oliver: THE GREAT LAKES. New York, 1900.

Cuthbertson, George A.: FRESHWATER. Toronto, 1931.

Disturnell, J.: SAILING ON THE GREAT LAKES. Philadelphia, 1874.

Fay, Charles Edey: MARY CELESTE. Salem, 1942.

The Fisherman: Current monthly magazine. Grand Haven.

Freeman, L. R.: BY WATERWAYS TO GOTHAM. New York, 1925.

Great Lakes News, The: Current magazine. Cleveland.

Great Lakes Red Book, The: Current Directory. Cleveland.

Great Lakes Review, The: Current magazine. Cleveland.

MEMORIES OF THE LAKES

Green's Marine Directory: Current. Cleveland.

Hatcher, Harlan: LAKE ERIE. Indianapolis, 1945.

Havighurst, Walter: THE LONG SHIPS PASSING. New York, 1942.

Hills, Norman E.: HISTORY OF KELLEYS ISLAND Toledo, 1925.

Holbrook, Stewart: IRON BREW. New York, 1940.

Horton, John L.: GREAT LAKES SEAMANSHIP. Vermilion, 1942.

Huron Institute Papers and Records: Collingwood, 1914.

Inland Seas: Current Bulletin, Cleveland.

Ireland, Tom: THE GREAT LAKES—ST. LAWRENCE DEEP WATERWAY TO THE SEA. New York, 1934.

Lake Carriers' Association Annual Report: Current. Cleveland.

Landon, Fred: LAKE HURON. Indianapolis, 1944.

Martin, Helen M.: NE-SAW-JE-WON. Cleveland, 1939.

McDougall, Alexander: AUTOBIOGRAPHY. Duluth, 1932.

Mills, James Cooke: OUR INLAND SEAS. Chicago, 1910.

Nichols' Handy Guide Book of Put-inBay, Middle Bass and Kelleys Island: Sandusky, 1888.

280

BIBLIOGRAPHY

Nute, Grace Lee: LAKE SUPERIOR. Indianapolis, 1944.

Plumb, Ralph G.: LAKE MICHIGAN. Manitowoc, 1941.

Port Light: Current Paper. Sturgeon Bay.

Pound, Arthur: LAKE ONTARIO. Indianapolis, 1945.

Quick, Herbert: AMERICAN INLAND WATERWAYS. New York, 1909.

Quaife, Milo M.: LAKE MICHIGAN. Indianapolis, 1944.

Ryall, Lydia J.: LAKE ERIE ISLANDS. Norwalk, 1913.

Ryan, James A.: THE TOWN OF MILAN. Sandusky, 1912.

SCOTT'S NEW COAST PILOT: Detroit, 1902.

SHIPMASTERS' ASSOCIATION DIRECTORY: Current. Cleveland.

STEAMBOAT BILL-OF-FACTS: Current magazine. Salem.

Trimble, George: THE LAKE PILOTS' HANDBOOK. Port Huron, 1907.

Waldron, Webb and Marion Patton: WE EXPLORE THE GREAT LAKES. New York, 1923.

Williams, Ralph D.: THE HONORABLE PETER WHITE. Cleveland, 1907.

DISTANCES BETWEEN POINTS ON LAKE SUPERIOR

Other tables to which initial points Nos. 1-4 are common:

III—Lake Michigan.
III—Lake Huron and St. Marys River.
IV—Lake Erie, St. Clair, Detroit, and Niagara Rivers.
VI—Lake Ontario and St. Lawrence River.

Initial / listed points:

1. Port Colborne (VI)
2. Port Huron (V)
3. Old Mackinac Point (III)
4. Sault Ste. Marie (IV)
5. Whitefish Point
6. Grand Marais, Mich.
7. Munising
8. Marquette (docks)
9. Huron Bay (village)
10. L'Anse
11. Mendota Canal
12. Copper Harbor
13. Eagle Harbor
14. Portage Entry
15. Chassell
16. Lake Linden
17. Dollar Bay
18. Houghton
19. Keweenaw Waterway Upper Entry
20. Ontonagon
21. Ashland
22. Washburn
23. Bayfield
24. Port Wing
25. Superior
26. Duluth
27. Two Harbors
28. Grand Marais, Minn.
29. Rock of Ages
30. Passage Island
31. Fort William
32. Port Arthur
33. Rossport
34. Peninsula Harbor
35. Quebec Harbor
36. Michipicoten Harbor
37. Gargantua Harbor

EXPLANATION

Explanation generally applicable to all tables is published in Table I.

Points in this table are arranged in geographical sequence proceeding westward along the south shore and returning eastward around the north shore.

For determining distances to points located in other lakes, distances from all places listed in this table are given to the initial points Nos. 1 to 4, which also appear in the other tables respectively indicated by numeral designation. The through distance from a given point in this table to a given point in any other table is the sum of the respective distances to each given point from the initial point which is common to the two tables. Thus, Port Huron being the common point for determining distances from Lake Superior points to points in Lake Erie (Table V), a through distance would be derived as follows:

Port Huron to Ontonagon 544
Port Huron to Dunkirk 292
                                        ——
Ontonagon to Dunkirk 836

*From foot of Grand River Ave.
*From sailing course point north of light.
*From abreast east end of United States center pier
*Via Keweenaw Waterway.

—Courtesy U. S. Lake Survey Office.

DISTANCES BETWEEN POINTS ON LAKE MICHIGAN

Other tables to which initial point No. 1 is common:

II—Lake Superior.
IV—Lake Huron and St. Marys River.
V—Lake Erie, St. Clair, Detroit, and Niagara Rivers.
VI—Lake Ontario and St. Lawrence River.

Distances (in the table the destination point is listed with the distances from each preceding point, 1 through n−1):

No.	Point	Distances from points 1 … (n−1)
1	Old Mackinac Point (II-IV-V-VI) *	—
2	Manistique	75
3	Escanaba	129, 60
4	Menominee b	155, 92, 55
5	Green Bay (city) b	198, 135, 100, 49
6	Sturgeon Bay (town)	155, 103, 90, 22, 47
7	Algoma	161, 111, 90, 43, 68, 21
8	Kewaunee	170, 120, 99, 52, 78, 81, 12
9	Two Rivers	187, 142, 101, 75, 101, 58, 36, 28
10	Manitowoc	191, 146, 106, 81, 108, 106, 40, 31, 6
11	Sheboygan	212, 168, 128, 62, 53, 55, 26
12	Port Washington	237, 195, 155, 130, 155, 129, 89, 79, 33, 29
13	Milwaukee	269, 220, 180, 133, 115, 105, 79, 65, 39
14	Racine	272, 235, 217, 172, 197, 123, 122, 100, 97, 74, 48, 26
15	Kenosha	252, 244, 228, 184, 209, 162, 142, 133, 109, 107, 58, 48, 14
16	Waukegan	296, 209, 242, 198, 223, 176, 158, 149, 125, 123, 74, 51, 31, 18
17	Chicago	324, 290, 274, 230, 255, 209, 198, 176, 156, 134, 85, 64, 54, 38
18	South Chicago	333, 298, 283, 240, 265, 218, 200, 181, 168, 166, 95, 75, 64, 54, 49, 15
19	Indiana Harbor	334, 301, 286, 243, 268, 222, 203, 194, 171, 169, 121, 99, 78, 67, 52, 19, 7
20	Gary	336, 303, 288, 246, 272, 225, 206, 197, 174, 173, 125, 103, 82, 71, 56, 13
21	Michigan City	325, 280, 260, 239, 264, 217, 200, 190, 167, 169, 124, 104, 83, 72, 58, 31, 22
22	St. Joseph	300, 255, 235, 216, 242, 195, 179, 170, 151, 150, 112, 96, 75, 70, 60, 39, 55, 36
23	South Haven	281, 250, 238, 200, 225, 178, 163, 137, 137, 123, 93, 80, 77, 79, 77, 57
24	Saugatuck	263, 232, 220, 183, 209, 162, 148, 123, 123, 97, 90, 89, 90, 95, 75, 44, 24
25	Holland	257, 226, 213, 177, 202, 155, 142, 118, 118, 94, 88, 85, 82, 93, 82, 49, 29, 8
26	Grand Haven	238, 213, 195, 159, 184, 137, 123, 101, 102, 78, 83, 80, 87, 114, 100, 99, 25, 21
27	Muskegon	234, 195, 151, 146, 171, 124, 111, 89, 90, 77, 80, 87, 120, 108, 120, 34, 13
28	White Lake	213, 170, 135, 159, 113, 100, 114, 78, 69, 72, 80, 88, 120, 114, 127, 45, 25, 13
29	Pentwater	184, 141, 108, 87, 75, 70, 61, 64, 63, 78, 91, 108, 77, 57, 46, 35
30	Ludington	173, 130, 98, 76, 66, 57, 60, 60, 80, 97, 117, 130, 157, 146, 154
31	Manistee	150, 112, 87, 65, 59, 58, 62, 66, 98, 117, 129, 138, 152, 179, 188, 191, 181
32	Portage Lake	142, 110, 80, 58, 59, 60, 75, 79, 96, 104, 125, 137, 147, 140, 108
33	Frankfort	110, 106, 86, 64, 60, 67, 71, 77, 83
34	Traverse City	94, 91, 120, 173, 143, 160, 164, 182, 160, 228, 242, 252, 266, 304, 309, 304, 268, 250, 227, 206, 195, 184, 154, 143, 118, 110
35	Charlevoix	56, 64, 99, *119, 176, 113, 119, 126, 142, 147, 165, 189, 211, 225, 234
36	Petoskey	55, 58, 18, *134, 181, 205, 135, 153, 159, 163, 181, 205, 227, 241, 251, 265, 293, 301, 303, 308, 294, 268, 250, 231, 225, 205, 194, 183, 153, 142, 117, 109, 92, 58, 18
37	Beaver Island Harbor	41, 43, 99, *122, *165, 123, 131, 138, 156, 161, 180, 206, 228, 242, 252, 266, 294, 302, 304, 309, 295, 269, 251, 232, 227, 205, 195, 184, 154, 143, 118, 110, 92, 69, 33, 37, 0

* From sailing course point north of light.
b Distances from Menominee and Green Bay to Lake Michigan points (except those marked *) are via Sturgeon Bay Canal.
* Via Rock Island Passage.

EXPLANATION

Explanation generally applicable to all tables is published in Table I.

Points in this table are arranged in geographical sequence proceeding southward along the west shore and returning northward along the east shore.

For determining distances to points in other lakes, distances from all places listed in this table are given to Old Mackinac Point, and this initial point also appears in each of the other tables respectively indicated by numeral designation. The through distance from a given point in this table to a given point in any other table is the sum of the respective distances to each given point from Old Mackinac Point, common to the two tables. Thus, a through distance from a Lake Michigan point to a point in Lake Superior (Table II) would be derived as follows:

Old Mackinac Point to Racine............... 272
Old Mackinac Point to Ashland.............. 439
                                          _____
Racine to Ashland.......................... 711

—Courtesy U. S. Lake Survey Office.

DISTANCES BETWEEN POINTS ON LAKE HURON AND ST. MARYS RIVER

Other tables to which initial points Nos. 1-3 are common:
II—Lake Superior.
III—Lake Michigan.
V—Lake Erie, St. Clair, Detroit, and Niagara Rivers.
VI—Lake Ontario and St. Lawrence River.

No.	Place	36 Thessalon	35 Algoma Mills	34 Gore Bay	33 Little Current	32 Killarney	31 French River	30 Key Harbor	29 Byng Inlet	28 Parry Sound	27 Depot Harbor	26 Victoria Harbor	25 Midland	24 Penetanguishene	23 Collingwood	22 Meaford	21 Owen Sound	20 Wiarton	19 Southampton	18 Kincardine	17 Goderich	16 Port Sanilac	15 Harbor Beach	14 Saginaw	13 Bay City	12 East Tawas	11 Au Sable	10 Alpena	9 Rockport	8 Rogers	7 Cheboygan	6 Mackinac Island	5 St. Ignace	4 Detour	3 Sault Ste. Marie	2 Old Mackinac Point
1	Port Huron (V-VI) [a]	*238	†238	†250	225	213	224	232	229	247	243	267	266	265	258	241	238	228	121	94	65	33	63	175	162	119	117	157	166	194	233	243	247	224	269	247
2	Old Mackinac Point (III) [b]	69	*101	*116	*143	*167	*196	*205	*211	235	231	256	255	254	247	230	227	217	189	192	211	215	186	223	210	163	142	115	83	54	18	7	6	45	90	
3	Sault Ste. Marie (II) [c]	‡48	‡88	‡106	‡131	‡155	‡184	‡193	‡201	‡242	‡238	268	267	266	259	242	239	229	207	213	234	238	208	246	232	185	165	137	107	84	84	84	90	45		
4	Detour	§24	§58	§76	§101	§125	§154	§163	§171	201	198	224	222	221	214	197	194	185	162	168	189	193	164	201	187	140	120	92	61	40	39	39	44			
5	St. Ignace	§68	*100	*115	*142	*166	*195	*204	*209	234	231	256	254	252	246	229	227	217	191	194	214	216	187	224	210	163	143	115	83	55	20	6				
6	Mackinac Island	§63	*95	*110	*137	*161	*190	*199	*204	229	226	251	249	248	241	224	221	212	186	189	209	212	184	220	207	159	140	111	79	50	17					
7	Cheboygan	§63	*92	*106	*133	*157	*186	*195	*197	221	217	242	241	240	233	216	213	204	175	178	198	202	173	210	196	149	129	101	69	40						
8	Rogers	*63	†74	†87	†114	†138	157	163	164	187	183	208	206	206	199	182	177	169	139	142	161	163	134	171	157	110	90	61	31							
9	Rockport	*79	†79	†92	†119	123	136	143	143	166	162	187	186	185	178	161	158	148	112	113	132	134	106	142	129	82	62	31								
10	Alpena	*107	†107	†120	†143	131	145	151	152	174	171	195	193	192	185	168	165	156	109	107	124	125	97	129	116	69	49									
11	Au Sable	*135	†135	†148	158	146	160	163	166	183	180	204	202	201	189	177	174	165	98	85	93	86	58	83	69	21										
12	East Tawas	*155	†155	†168	175	163	176	180	182	199	196	220	218	217	210	194	190	181	110	94	95	88	60	68	54											
13	Bay City	*202	†202	†215	222	210	223	223	229	245	243	267	265	264	257	240	237	228	153	136	137	130	102	13												
14	Saginaw	*216	†216	†228	235	223	237	242	242	258	256	280	278	278	271	254	250	241	167	149	151	144	115													
15	Harbor Beach	*178	†178	†191	171	159	171	176	176	194	190	214	213	212	205	188	185	175	79	56	47	32														
16	Port Sanilac	*207	†207	†219	197	185	196	201	201	219	215	239	238	237	230	213	210	200	97	70	47															
17	Goderich	†198	†198	204	169	159	172	172	174	192	189	213	211	210	207	187	183	174	64	36																
18	Kincardine	†173	†174	174	141	128	142	149	144	162	158	182	181	180	176	156	153	144	30																	
19	Southampton	†166	†166	155	122	110	123	130	125	143	140	163	162	161	157	137	134	125																		
20	Wiarton [d]	†188	158	142	110	94	88	79	81	74	71	76	74	73	53	36	29																			
21	Owen Sound [d]	†197	167	152	119	103	97	97	89	79	75	71	70	69	46	29																				
22	Meaford [d]	†200	169	153	121	105	96	96	86	71	68	55	53	52	24																					
23	Collingwood [d]	†217	186	171	138	120	108	107	97	80	76	57	55	54																						
24	Penetanguishene [d]	†224	187	172	139	120	106	104	94	72	69	12	10																							
25	Midland [d]	†225	188	173	140	121	107	105	95	73	70	7																								
26	Port McNicoll [d]	†227	190	174	142	122	108	106	97	75	71																									
27	Depot Harbor [d]	193	155	140	107	87	73	71	62	6																										
28	Parry Sound [d]	197	159	143	111	91	77	75	65																											
29	Byng Inlet [d]	155	118	102	70	50	31	27																												
30	Key Harbor [d]	148	110	94	62	42	22																													
31	French River [d]	139	101	86	53	33																														
32	Killarney [d]	110	72	56	24																															
33	Little Current	86	48	33																																
34	Gore Bay	61	27																																	
35	Algoma Mills	43																																		
36	Thessalon	0																																		

[a] From foot of Grand River Ave.

[b] From sailing course point north of light.

[c] From abreast east end of U. S. center pier, and (except those marked ‡) via Middle Neebish and Detour; distances downbound through West Neebish are 1 mile less.

[d] Distances to Georgian Bay ports (except those marked *, †, ‡, §) are via the bay entrance from Lake Huron and St. Marys River points and via Little Current from North Channel points.

* Via False Detour and North Channels.
† Via Mississagi Strait and North Channel.
‡ Via Hay Lake, St. Joseph, and North Channels.
§ Via Potagannissing Bay and North Channel.

EXPLANATION

Explanation generally applicable to all tables is published in Table I.

Points in this table are arranged in geographical sequence proceeding from St. Marys River southward along the west shore, and returning northward up the east shore, around Georgian Bay, and westward through North Channel.

For determining distances to points located in other lakes, distances from all places listed in this table are given to the initial points Nos. 1 to 3, which also appear in the other tables respectively indicated by numeral designation. The through distance from a given point in this table to a given point in any other table is the sum of the respective distances to each given point from the initial point which is common to the two tables.

DISTANCES BETWEEN POINTS ON LAKE ERIE AND ST. CLAIR, DETROIT, AND NIAGARA RIVERS

Other tables to which initial points Nos. 1–3 are common:
II—Lake Superior.
III—Lake Michigan.
IV—Lake Huron and St. Marys River.
VI—Lake Ontario and St. Lawrence River.

Column (destination) reference numbers and points:

2	Port Colborne
3	Port Huron
4	St. Clair
5	Marine City
6	Algonac
7	St. Clair Flats
8	Mt. Clemens
9	Chatham
10	Detroit
11	Wyandotte
12	Trenton
13	Amherstburg
14	Detroit River Light
15	Monroe
16	Toledo
17	Port Clinton
18	Put-in-Bay
19	Sandusky
20	Huron
21	Vermilion
22	Lorain
23	Cleveland
24	Fairport
25	Ashtabula
26	Conneaut
27	Erie
28	Dunkirk
29	Buffalo
30	Tonawanda
31	Niagara Falls
32	Port Maitland
33	Port Dover
34	Port Burwell
35	Port Stanley
36	Rondeau
37	Kingsville

Row (origin) points 1–37:

1	Old Mackinac Point (III) a
2	Port Colborne (VI)
3	Port Huron (II–IV) a
4	St. Clair
5	Marine City
6	Algonac
7	St. Clair Flats a
8	Mt. Clemens
9	Chatham
10	Detroit (Woodward Ave.) b
11	Wyandotte
12	Trenton
13	Amherstburg
14	Detroit River Light
15	Monroe (piers)
16	Toledo (river mouth)
17	Port Clinton
18	Put-in-Bay
19	Sandusky (wharves)
20	Huron
21	Vermilion
22	Lorain
23	Cleveland (main entrance)
24	Fairport
25	Ashtabula
26	Conneaut
27	Erie
28	Dunkirk
29	Buffalo
30	Tonawanda
31	Niagara Falls
32	Port Maitland
33	Port Dover
34	Port Burwell
35	Port Stanley
36	Rondeau
37	Kingsville

Distances (origin row × destination column; upper-triangular):

Origin \ Dest	2	3	4	5	6	7	8	9	10	11	12	13	14	15	16	17	18	19	20	21	22	23	24	25	26	27	28	29	30	31	32	33	34	35	36	37
1 Old Mackinac Pt.	553	247	259	265	274	286	296	322	309	320	324	326	334	348	363	369	363	380	387	391	399	417	435	460	473	500	539	569	580	588	538	527	475	459	414	338
2 Port Colborne		306	294	287	281	267	278	292	244	229	229	227	219	227	237	213	204	204	198	190	180	160	130	104	92	65	25	22	33	41	18	52	89	109	146	201
3 Port Huron			12	19	27	39	49	75	62	77	77	79	87	101	116	122	116	133	140	144	152	151	170	213	226	253	292	322	333	341	291	280	228	212	167	111
4 St. Clair				7	15	27	37	62	50	60	58	60	73	89	105	111	105	122	129	133	141	149													159	99
5 Marine City					7	20	30	56	43	54	53	58	68	82	97	97	92	118	125	129	128														148	92
6 Algonac						14	22	33	37	45	45	53	62	76	92	93	98	109	116	120	109															86
7 St. Clair Flats							15	35	23	30	30	41	48	62	78	89	84	95	102	106	114															72
8 Mt. Clemens								49	35	45	48	53	58	73	89	95	95	106	113	117	125															53
9 Chatham									48	59	59	59	73	87	102	108	108	120	127	130	139															97
10 Detroit										11	16	18	25	39	54	54	42	72	64	73	91															49
11 Wyandotte											5	8	20	29	45	45	43	62	60	68	82															39
12 Trenton												13	15	24	40	40	35	57	54	60	73															34
13 Amherstburg													7	21	36	36	30	54	61	64	72															31
14 Det. River Light														14	30	30	27	47	54	55	43															24
15 Monroe															21	21	21	48	48	54	38															33
16 Toledo																40	12	52	36	32	29															45
17 Port Clinton																	38	22	22	29	20															37
18 Put-in-Bay																		21	11	20	11															27
19 Sandusky																			14	11	14															41
20 Huron																				11																49
21 Vermilion																																				46
22 Lorain																																				48
23 Cleveland																										28										65
24 Fairport																									33	33	44									83
25 Ashtabula																										30	39								125	108
26 Conneaut																											15									122
27 Erie																											45	37								149
28 Dunkirk																												45	13	8						188
29 Buffalo																													13		57					218
30 Tonawanda																														8						230
31 Niagara Falls																																				182
32 Port Maitland																																57				187
33 Port Dover																																	37			175
34 Port Burwell																																		23		123
35 Port Stanley																																			40	108
36 Rondeau																																				63
37 Kingsville																																				0

a From sailing course point north of light.
b From foot of Grand River Ave.
c From south end of canal dike.

EXPLANATION

Explanation generally applicable to all tables is published in Table I.

Points in this table are arranged in geographical sequence proceeding southward in St. Clair River and Lake and Detroit River, eastward along the south shore of Lake Erie to Niagara River, and returning westward along the north lake shore.

For determining distances to points located in other lakes, distances from all places listed in this table are given to the initial points Nos. 1 to 3, which also appear in the other tables respectively indicated by numeral designation. The through distance from a given point in this table to a given point in any other table is the sum of the respective distances to each given point from the initial point which is common to the two tables. Thus, Old Mackinac Point being the common point for determining distances from Lake Erie to points in Lake Michigan (Table III), a through distance would be derived as follows:

Old Mackinac Point to Tonawanda.......... 580
Old Mackinac Point to Sheboygan.......... 212

Tonawanda to Sheboygan.................. 792

—Courtesy U. S. Lake Survey Office.

DISTANCES BETWEEN POINTS ON LAKE ONTARIO AND ST. LAWRENCE RIVER

Other table to which initial points Nos. 1-3 are common:

II—Lake Superior.
III—Lake Michigan.
IV—Lake Huron and St. Marys River.
V—Lake Erie, St. Clair, Detroit, and Niagara Rivers.

Distances (in statute miles) from the three initial points to each listed point:

No.	Point	Old Mackinac Point (III)	Port Huron (IV)	Port Colborne (II–V)
3	Port Colborne	553	305	—
4	Cape Vincent	740	493	187
5	Sacketts Harbor	745	498	192
6	Oswego	721	474	168
7	Little Sodus Bay	712	465	159
8	Sodus Bay	698	451	145
9	Rochester (Charlotte)	670	423	117
10	Olcott	608	361	55
11	Niagara-on-the-Lake	592	345	39
12	Lewiston	598	351	57
13	Port Weller	580	333	27
14	Hamilton	610	363	57
15	Toronto (east entrance)	608	361	55
16	Port Hope	648	401	106
17	Cobourg	653	406	101
18	Trenton	688	441	135
19	Belleville	697	450	144
20	Deseronto	713	466	160
21	Picton	728	479	173
22	Kingston	739	492	186
23	Gananoque	758	511	205
24	Clayton	755	508	202
25	Thousand Island Park	760	513	207
26	Alexandria Bay	766	519	211
27	Brockville	787	540	232
28	Ogdensburg	799	552	244
29	Galop Canal	806	559	251
30	Rapide Flat Canal	817	570	264
31	Farran Point Canal	831	584	278
32	Cornwall Canal	836	589	283
33	Cornwall	847	600	294
34	St. Regis	831	604	298
35	Soulanges Canal	878	631	325
36	Lachine Canal	908	661	355
37	Montreal	917	670	364

Initial points:
1 — Old Mackinac Point (III)
2 — Port Huron (IV)
3 — Port Colborne (II–V)

(A triangular matrix of the intervening distances between each pair of the numbered points 4–37 is printed on this page; selected near-diagonal values include: Cape Vincent–Sacketts Harbor 26; Oswego–Little Sodus Bay 15; Little Sodus Bay–Sodus Bay 18; Niagara-on-the-Lake–Lewiston 6; Cobourg–Trenton 7; Belleville–Deseronto 17; Kingston–Gananoque 19; Clayton–Thousand Island Park 4; Thousand Island Park–Alexandria Bay 8; Alexandria Bay–Brockville 22; Ogdensburg–Galop Canal 7; Rapide Flat Canal–Farran Point Canal 11; Farran Point Canal–Cornwall Canal 13; Cornwall–St. Regis 6; St. Regis–Soulanges Canal 29; Soulanges Canal–Lachine Canal 29.)

* From sailing course point north of light.
♭ From foot of Grand River Ave.
° From upper end of canal.
◦ To Toronto west entrance.

Points in this table are arranged in geographical sequence proceeding westward along the south shore and returning eastward along the north shore of the lake and down St. Lawrence River.

For determining distances to points located in other lakes, distances from all places listed in this table are given to the initial points Nos. 1 to 3, which also appear in the other tables respectively indicated by numeral designation. The through distance from a given point in this table to a given point in any other table is the sum of the respective distances to each given point from the initial point which is common to the two tables. Thus, Port Colborne being the common point for determining distances from Lake Ontario and St. Lawrence River points to points in Lake Superior (Table II), a through distance would be derived as follows:

Port Colborne to Cornwall............ 294
Port Colborne to Fort William....... 847

Cornwall to Fort William............ 1,141

EXPLANATION

Explanation generally applicable to all tables is published in Table I.

INDEX OF SHIPS

Note: * Indicates Pictorial Section

Note: * Indicates Pictorial Section

INDEX OF SHIPS — (Continued)

Note: * Indicates Pictorial Section

289

Note: * Indicates Pictorial Section

Note: * Indicates Pictorial Section

INDEX OF SHIPS — (Continued)

NOTES

NOTES

NOTES

NOTES

NOTES

NOTES

NOTES

NOTES

NOTES

NOTES